Twitter: A Digital Socioscope

How can Twitter data be used to study individual-level human behavior and social inter-action on a global scale? This book introduces readers to the methods, opportunities, and challenges of using Twitter data to analyze phenomena ranging from the number of people infected by the flu, to national elections, to tomorrow's stock prices. Each chapter, written by leading domain experts in clear and accessible language, takes the reader to the forefront of the newly emerging field of computational social science.

An introductory chapter on Twitter data analysis provides an overview of key tools and skills and gives pointers on how to get started, while the case studies demonstrate shortcomings, limitations, and pitfalls of Twitter data as well as their advantages. The book will be an excellent resource for social science students and researchers wanting to explore the use of online data.

YELENA MEJOVA is a scientist in the Social Computing Group at Qatar Computing Research Institute (QCRI). Before joining QCRI, Yelena was a postdoc at Yahoo! Research in Barcelona. A part of the Web Mining Group, her work concerned building semantically enriched information retrieval systems, as well as examining user behavior through social media. Prior to that, her Ph.D. thesis at the University of Iowa concerned the design and application of sentiment analysis tools for mining a variety of social media discourses, including political speech.

INGMAR WEBER is a senior scientist in the Social Computing Group at QCRI. As an undergraduate, he studied mathematics at Cambridge University, UK, before moving to the Max Planck Institute for Computer Science, Germany, for his Ph.D. Before moving to Qatar, he spent two years working at the École Polytechnique Fédérale de Lausanne, Switzerland, and three years at Yahoo! Research in Barcelona.

MICHAEL W. MACY is Goldwin Smith Professor of Arts and Sciences and Director of the Social Dynamics Laboratory at Cornell University. His research team has used computational models, online experiments, and data from social media to explore enig-matic social patterns, the emergence and collapse of fads, the spread of self-destructive behaviors, cooperation in social dilemmas, the critical mass in collective action, the spread of contagions on small-world networks, the polarization of opinion, segregation of neighborhoods, and assimilation of minority cultures.

Twitter: A Digital Socioscope

Edited by

YELENA MEJOVA

Qatar Computing Research Institute

INGMAR WEBER

Qatar Computing Research Institute

MICHAEL W. MACY

Cornell University, Ithaca, New York

CAMBRIDGE
UNIVERSITY PRESS

CAMBRIDGE
UNIVERSITY PRESS

32 Avenue of the Americas, New York, NY 10013-2473, USA

Cambridge University Press is part of the University of Cambridge.

It furthers the University's mission by disseminating knowledge in the pursuit of
education, learning, and research at the highest international levels of excellence.

www.cambridge.org
Information on this title: www.cambridge.org/9781107500075

First published 2015

Printed in the United States of America

A catalog record for this publication is available from the British Library.

Library of Congress Cataloging in Publication Data
Twitter : a digital socioscope / [edited by] Yelena Mejova, Ingmar Weber, Michael W. Macy.
pages   cm
Includes bibliographical references and index.
ISBN 978-1-107-10237-8 (hardback) – ISBN 978-1-107-50007-5 (paperback)
1. Twitter.   2. Dyadic data analysis (Social sciences)   3. Online social networks –
Research.   4. Social sciences – Research – Methodology.   5. Webometrics.   I. Mejova,
Yelena, 1985–   II. Weber, Ingmar, 1978–   III. Macy, Michael W.
HM533.5.T95   2015
302.34072′7–dc23   2015003326

ISBN 978-1-107-10237-8 Hardback
ISBN 978-1-107-50007-5 Paperback

Contents

Contributors

Mark Cameron *Senior Research Scientist in the Digital Productivity Flagship of the Commonwealth Scientific and Industrial Research Organisation*

Daniel Gayo-Avello *Associate Professor in the Department of Computer Science at the University of Oviedo*

Scott A. Golder *Ph.D. candidate in Sociology at Cornell University and Data Scientist and Staff Sociologist at the Context Relevant Department of Sociology, Cornell University*

Patty Kostkova *Principal Research Associate in e-Health at University College London*

Shamanth Kumar *Ph.D. candidate in Computer Science and Engineering at Arizona State University*

Huan Liu *Professor of Computer Science and Engineering at Arizona State University*

Michael W. Macy *Goldwin Smith Professor of Arts and Sciences and Director of the Social Dynamics Laboratory at Cornell University*

Huina Mao *Ph.D. candidate at the School of Informatics and Computing at Indiana University*

Fred Morstatter *Ph.D. student in Computer Science and Engineering at Arizona State University*

Robert Power *Team Leader in the Digital Productivity Flagship of the Commonwealth Scientific and Industrial Research Organisation*

Daniele Quercia *College Research Associate, University of Cambridge*

Bella Robinson *Senior Software Engineer in the Digital Productivity Flagship of the Commonwealth Scientific and Industrial Research Organisation*

Preface

More than 500 million tweets are shared on Twitter each day, each devoting 140 characters to anything from announcements of dinner plans to calls for revolutions. Given its sheer size and the fact that most of its content is public, it is not surprising that Twitter has been extensively used to study human behavior on a global scale.

This book uses thematically grouped case studies to show how Twitter data can be used to analyze phenomena ranging from the number of people infected by the flu, to national elections, to tomorrow's stock prices. The idea for the book grew out of a three-hour tutorial on "Twitter and the Real World" given in October 2013 at the Conference on Information and Knowledge Management. Expanding on the topics covered in that tutorial, the book provides a wider thematic scope of research and the most recent scientific work.

All chapters are written by leading domain experts and take the reader to the forefront of the emerging new field of computational social science, using topical applications to illustrate the possibilities, advantages, and limitations of large, semistructured social media data to gain insights into human behavior and social interaction. Although most of the authors are computer scientists, the book is intended for readers who have not been exposed to formal training on how to analyze "big data." To this end, unnecessary implementation details are avoided. Chapter 1, "Analyzing Twitter Data," introduces readers to the tools and skills used in these studies and gives pointers on how to take the first steps as a novice researcher.

The opening chapter lays the groundwork for the book by surveying the opportunities and challenges of a "Twitter socioscope." The chapters that follow are written to be stand-alone case studies that can be reordered according to the reader's needs and preferences.

Twitter will undoubtedly evolve and its usage will change, but even if it comes to be replaced by "the next big thing," the detailed time-stamped records of hundreds of millions of global users will continue to be one of the most valuable sources of data on human behavior ever assembled, and these case studies will remain useful as an introduction to the methods, research opportunities, and challenges that these data present.

Finally, we would like to thank all the chapter authors for their hard work to ensure the highest quality and timeliness of this book.

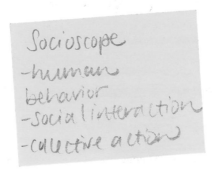

Introduction

Scott A. Golder and Michael W. Macy

[J]ust as the invention of the telescope revolutionized the study of the heavens, so too by rendering the unmeasurable measurable, the technological revolution in mobile, Web, and Internet communications has the potential to revolutionize our understanding of ourselves and how we interact... [T]hree hundred years after Alexander Pope argued that the proper study of mankind should lie not in the heavens but in ourselves, we have finally found our telescope. Let the revolution begin....

– Duncan Watts (2012, p. 266)

Online interaction is now a regular part of daily life for a demographically diverse population of billions of people worldwide. Facebook and Twitter are two of the most popular places where these interactions take place. A key difference is that most content on Twitter is publicly accessible via the Twitter API or through data resellers such as GNIP and Datasift, whereas most Facebook content is private. Thus, Twitter has emerged as the single most powerful "socioscope" available to social scientists for collecting fine-grained time-stamped records of human behavior and social interaction at the level of individual events. These data are also global in scale, allowing researchers to address fundamental questions about social identity, status, conflict, cooperation, collective action, and diffusion. This unprecedented opportunity comes with a number of methodological challenges, including generalizing observations to the offline world, protecting individual privacy, and solving the logistical challenges posed by "big data." This introductory chapter reviews current advances in online social research and critically assesses the theoretical and methodological opportunities and limitations.

This chapter is condensed from a larger survey of social media studies published in the *Annual Review of Sociology*. The material is included here with the permission of the publisher.

Opportunities and Challenges for Online Social Research

Scientific disciplines make revolutionary advances not only through new discoveries, theories, and paradigms, but also because of the invention of new tools and methodologies (Kuhn, 1962). The electron microscope, space telescope, particle accelerator, and magnetic resonance imaging (MRI) have allowed scientists to observe the world at greater scale or at finer resolution, revealing previously obscured details and unexpected patterns and experiencing the "eureka moments" of scientific breakthroughs. Newly developed tools for observing online activity are having a similar transformative effect on the social and behavioral sciences. Recent studies show how "digital footprints" collected from online communities and networks enable us to understand human behavior and social interaction in ways we could not do before. While the societal impact of electronic communication is widely recognized, its impact on social and behavioral science is also profound, providing global yet fine-grained observational data and a locus for population-scale experimentation.

Hard Science

Over the past century, there has been no shortage of social theory, but there are severe constraints on access to data. The reason is simple: social life is very hard to observe. For example, it is much easier to ask an isolated individual about their friends than to observe the ongoing interactions and exchanges that are the stuff of friendship. Ethnographic participant-observation studies and surveys of complete networks make it possible to fully document social interactions, but only at costs that can be prohibitively expensive to implement except in very small groups. The need to collect relational data through direct contact has therefore generally limited studies of social interactions to small, bounded groups such as clubs (Zachary, 1977) and villages (Entwisle et al., 2007). Lengthy time-series data on large populations, such as the Framingham Heart Study[1] or the National Longitudinal Study of Adolescent Health (Harris et al., 2009) are enormously expensive logistical challenges and are usually undertaken by multiple cooperating institutions in government and academia. Attempts to measure network structure at the population level by surveying egocentric networks (a randomly chosen person and his or

---

[1]   http://www.framinghamheartstudy.org.

her network neighbors) can be useful for studying the attributes of network nodes (such as degree) and edges (such as tie strength), but this methodology has serious limitations (Marsden, 1990; Flynn, Reagans, & Guillory, 2010), including the inability to measure essential network attributes (e.g., distances, clustering, connectivity, and centrality) or social interactions (e.g., diffusion and polarization).

Because of the difficulty observing social interactions at population scale, most surveys rely on random samples composed of observations that are selected to be independent and to provide an unbiased representation of the underlying population distribution. However, independent observations preclude the ability to directly measure influence from a respondent's friends. We know that people do not entirely "think for themselves," but when we study opinion formation using random samples, we are left with little choice but to assume that a respondent's opinions are shaped entirely by his or her other traits, such as demographic background, material self-interest, or personal experience. As a result, we cannot rule out the possibility that demographic differences in opinions (e.g., the social liberalism of college graduates) are spuriously generated or exaggerated by the unmeasured effects of peer influence (McPherson 2004; Salganik, Dodds, & Watts, 2006; Della Posta, Shi, & Macy, 2013). Conversely, snowball sampling makes it possible to obtain relational data among network neighbors with which to measure demographic differences in beliefs and behavior net of the similarity between network neighbors, but the path dependence in selecting respondents makes it more difficult to obtain an unbiased representation of the population distribution.

Longstanding limitations on the ability to observe social interaction are rapidly disappearing as people all over the globe are increasingly choosing to interact using devices that provide detailed relational records. Data from online social networks – email archives, phone logs, text messages, and social media postings – allow researchers to relax the atomistic assumptions that are imposed by reliance on random samples. In place of path analytic models of social life as relationships among variables that measure individual traits (Wright, 1934; Duncan, 1966), data from online social networks makes it possible to model social life as relationships among actors (Macy & Willer, 2002).

Among these networks, Twitter stands out as by far the largest and most comprehensive publicly accessible source of online data on human behavior and social interaction. Each day, Twitter users leave billions of time-stamped digital footprints of social interactions, affording unprecedented opportunities for the collection of observational data on a scale that is at once massive and microscopic – massive in the sense that the people under study can number into the hundreds of millions and the data grow into the terabytes, and microscopic in the sense that individual time-stamped microinteractions are recorded. In place of retrospective reports about respondents' behavior and interactions, Twitter data can provide a detailed record of daily activities and the frequency and intensity of social relationships. These methods greatly expand our ability to measure changes in behavior, not just opinion; to measure these changes at the individual level yet on a global scale that spans diverse cultures; to observe the structure of the underlying social network in which these individuals are embedded; to travel back in time to track the lead-up to what later becomes an event of interest; and to find the "dogs that don't bark" (e.g., the failed outcomes that escape the attention of publishers, editors, and authors).

This research strategy is not new. For many decades, social and behavioral scientists have acquired data collected as a byproduct of the administrative or record-keeping processes of governments and organizations. Organizations track their membership lists, firms track the purchases of customers and the performance of employees, and banks collect massive data from credit card transactions. What is new is the macroscopic global scale and microscopic behavioral extensiveness of the data that are becoming available for social and behavioral science. Every tweet resides in a data warehouse waiting to be mined for insights into behavior, and to enable useful functions from spam detection to product recommendations to targeted advertising.

The Social Telescope

The ability to observe hundreds of millions of global tweets makes it possible to measure differences with small effect sizes that might otherwise be swamped by random variability. Just as an enormous antenna such as the Arecibo Observatory is required to detect the low-frequency radiation emitted from neutron stars (Lovelace & Tyler, 2012), Twitter comprises a massive antenna for social science that makes visible both the very large (e.g., global patterns of communication densities between countries; State, Abrahao, & Cook, 2012) and the very small (e.g., hourly changes in emotional affect and microbehaviors such as doing homework, getting drunk, and getting a headache; Golder & Macy 2011).[2]

---

[2]   The associated website timeu.se (http://timeu.se/) provides an interactive tool for plotting the prevalence of keywords over the course of the day and week.

Tweets are recorded in real time rather than retrospectively. In social network studies, when individuals are given "name generators" and surveyed about their communication patterns, they are subject to a variety of potential biases. Question wording and ordering can cause respondents to artificially limit or otherwise vary the individuals they report, leading to underestimates of network size (Fischer, 2009; Pustejovsky & Spillane, 2009) or even measures of some other network (Burt, 1997) when survey questions mistakenly elicit report of a social tie outside the researcher's intended scope. In contrast, every tweet is time-stamped and passively recorded. If the message is retweeted, the data include not only the message content but also from whom the author may have received the message.

When activities are recorded via mobile devices, real-time geotagged mosaic accounts of collective behavior become possible that otherwise could not be reconstructed. As smartphone use increases in prevalence, the offline context of online behavior becomes available, such as common participation in a public event. For example, sampling a corpus of tweets that occurred during a certain time range and within a limited radius of a given event, we can reconstruct how online activity complemented a parade or demonstration or add a geographic variable back into an analysis that is otherwise blind to spatial location.

Relatedly, scientists can observe tweets unobtrusively, limiting the potential for Hawthorne-type effects in which researcher-induced desirability bias makes it difficult to observe normatively inappropriate behaviors (e.g., expressions of racial and ethnic prejudice), which participants may self-censor in surveys and in laboratory studies (Zizzo, 2010). Observing behavior unobtrusively ensures that the social pressures and normative constraints on individuals are exerted by their peers rather than by the researchers. Moreover, Twitter messages can be targeted to specific users with "@mentions," creating threaded conversations that can be observed in real time.

The task for the researcher is to see Twitter behavior as social behavior, the kind that might occur in any field site, be it a remote village, a law office, or a high school cafeteria. Some researchers explicitly conceptualize online sites as field sites in the ethnographic sense (Lyman & Wakeford, 1999). Relatedly, Twitter behavior represents social action in the Weberian sense – action that is oriented toward others (Weber, 1922), involving what Weber called "*verstehen*" – the subjective meaning for the actors involved. Paccagnella (1997) noted the multiple ways one might interpret the purpose, use, and limitations of technology, hence the need not to conflate the meaning to the researcher with the meaning for users (Pinch & Bijker, 1984).

Research Applications

Social Networks, Contagion, and Diffusion

Social network analyses have been among the earliest studies to use Twitter data. Twitter allows users to view indirectly the content received by those they follow only if the user also follows those same people.[3] In contrast to Facebook, which requires symmetric social ties (two friends must each indicate friendship with the other), Twitter (like most blogging platforms) allows asymmetric ties, leading to an extremely long-tailed degree distribution (e.g., celebrities often have many thousands of followers). Twitter also differs from Facebook by not demanding a clear tie to one's offline identity. Thus, the social network among Twitter users cannot be equated with an offline network based primarily on face-to-face interaction, as might exist in a school or workplace. Nevertheless, a recent study compared the volume and direction of messages, retweets, and @mentions among Twitter followers with the same users' offline friends and discovered a close correspondence (Xie et al., 2012).

Romero, Meeder, and Kleinberg (2011) found evidence to support the theory of complex contagions (Centola & Macy, 2007) by examining the spread of the use of Twitter hashtags. Hashtags for controversial topics such as politics were more likely to be adopted following exposure to multiple adopting neighbors, compared to topics such as music or sports. More recently, Weng, Menczer, and Ahn (2013) used Twitter hashtags to confirm a key implication of the theory of complex contagions – that the spread of complex contagions depends on network structure, a result that is consistent with the experimental findings reported by Centola (2010). Other studies have used online data to test longstanding theories about information diffusion, including the existence of well-connected "influentials" who initiate cascades. Popularized by Gladwell (2000) in *The Tipping Point*, the theory of these high-degree network nodes (or "hubs") was earlier proposed by Katz and Lazarsfeld (1955), who referred to them as "opinion leaders" in a two-step model of the flow of influence. Billions of advertising dollars are targeted at so-called influentials based on this theory, but a growing number of studies cast serious doubts. Cha et al.'s (2010) study of 1.7 billion tweets found that hubs "are not necessarily influential in terms of spawning retweets or mentions," a result consistent with Kwak et al. (2010), which also casts doubt on the influence of widely followed users on Twitter.

---

[3] That is, if A follows B, then A can see all of B's messages, but if B and C engage in a conversation, this is visible to A only if he follows both B and C. The purpose of this is more to prevent cluttering A's message stream with irrelevant conversations than to protect the privacy of B and C's conversation.

Using Twitter to measure the effectiveness of advertising is only one of several ways that these data have been used to study economic behavior. Chapter 3 of this volume shows how Twitter data have been used to measure unemployment, consumer confidence, social mood, investor sentiment, and the direction of financial markets. The chapter also refers to other sources for mining data for tracking and predicting economic behavior, including search queries and mobile phone data. The authors conclude by addressing the challenges that researchers face and identifying strategies for addressing these in future work.

Attention is also a valued resource in social exchange. Podolny (2001) suggests that attention is a prism or lens through which one is judged by others; having the attention of powerful others can, in turn, redound to one's financial benefit and is a signal to others about who is worth the investment of attention. Twitter users have been shown, for example, to rate others as more interesting to the extent that their own neighbors expressed interest in those others (Golder & Yardi, 2010).

In addition to social contagions, Twitter has also been used to track, study, and intervene in the spread of disease. Chapter 5 of this volume documents Twitter's strength as a public health medium for two-way communication, both as a health information source for users and also as a central hub for the collection and dissemination of health information that can improve early-warning and preparedness, aid disease prevalence mapping, and provide personally targeted health advice. Chapter 4 extends the research application from physical to emotional health, focusing on the use of Twitter data, in conjunction with census tract data, to study the ecological relationship between language use (e.g., sentiment analysis) and psychological experience.

Collective Action and Social Movements

Twitter data have also been used to study collective action and social movement mobilization. For example, data from Twitter have been used to provide digital traces of the spread of protest information and public sentiment in the Arab Spring (González-Bailón et al., 2011). Because information about protests reaches people through numerous channels besides social media, it is impossible to isolate the effects of social media net of other channels. However, users' messages can be used to measure the rate and extent of mobilization by tracking topic changes in user-generated content at a very fine-grained temporal level, and these changes can in turn be correlated with changes in the users' social and spatial environment as reflected in news accounts as well as the content of other users. For example, Weber, Garimella, and Batayneh (2013) track secular versus Islamist postings by Egyptian Twitter users over the course of the Arab Spring.

Twitter is not only a new channel for social movement organizers, but also for emergency managers to mobilize resources during disaster response and recovery activities. Chapter 6 of this volume extends research on mobilization to the responses of authorities to large-scale disasters. The chapter shows how Twitter has been used successfully to identify emergency events, obtain crowd-sourced information as the event unfolds, and provide up-to-date information to the affected community from authoritative agencies and for resource planning purposes.

Researchers have also used changes in the distribution of user-generated content not only to explain political outcomes but to try to predict them. For example, Digrazia et al. (2013) showed that local U.S. election outcomes were positively correlated with the number of times that Republicans had been mentioned in tweets. Nevertheless, a review of recent papers (Gayo-Avello, 2012) concluded that predictive claims are exaggerated. One important limitation on predictive power is that users of social media are not randomly selected in the way that is possible with survey research. Users preferentially choose to follow sources that conform to their existing worldviews (Sunstein, 2001) and preferentially rebroadcast ("retweet") conforming messages (Conover et al., 2011). Boutyline and Willer (2011) showed that there is a valence effect to the formation of so-called echo chambers – those further to the political right exhibited more ideological homophily in who they chose to follow on Twitter.

Chapter 2 of this volume uses representative case studies to show how Twitter data can be used to track public opinion through its expression in political discussions. The chapter also identifies challenging problems in measuring opinion and how these might be addressed in future research. These and other studies show that the use of social media to study opinion dynamics provides a potentially important complement to – not substitute for – traditional survey methods. Each can be used to obtain information that is missing in the other. Surveys provide more reliable estimates of the distribution of opinion in the underlying population but typically provide only retrospective responses and lack network data with which to study the flow, diffusion, and clustering of opinion.

Challenges

The Privacy Paradox

Twitter data confront researchers with imposing hurdles, ranging from validity of both the data and how they are sampled to the ethical issues regarding their use. Online data present a paradox in the protection of privacy: data are at once too revealing and not revealing enough. Twitter data lack the detailed demographic profile information that is standard in survey research. For example, while most Twitter data are public, profiles can also be private, and direct messages (which can only be sent to followers) are not world readable even for public profiles. Many users provide sparse, invented, incomplete, or ambiguous profile information, making it difficult for researchers to associate the content of tweets or the attributes of network nodes with basic demographic measures such as age, gender, ethnicity, or location. Identity is slippery and poorly defined in some online communities, where participants are known only by a self-chosen username that they may change at any time. In some cases, it is difficult to tell who is a human; the growing incidence of "spam accounts" is worrisome, and despite progress in spam detection methods (Yardi et al., 2010), spammers manage to keep the arms race going. As spammers become more sophisticated, it becomes harder for social scientists to clean the data they collect without specialized technical training, a problem we explore in more detail later.

Nevertheless, rapid progress is being made to address these limitations. For example, Compton et al. (2013) showed how label-propagation algorithms can be adapted to potentially geotag the vast majority of Twitter users to within a few kilometers, and Jernigan and Mistree (2009) (using Facebook data, although the method can also be applied to tweets) showed how social media content can be used to infer a wide range of user attributes, including age, gender, sexual preference, and political party affiliation. These advances illustrate the other side of the dilemma – that online data may not be private enough. These new sources of data raise challenging procedural, legal, and ethical questions about how to protect individual privacy that are beyond the scope of this review, but there is a growing body of research showing that anonymizing or encrypting data is not sufficient for protecting privacy, as this can sometimes be reverse-engineered (Backstrom, Dwork, & Kleinberg, 2007; de Montjoye et al., 2013) using the unique attributes of individuals' egocentric networks or physical mobility patterns.

Access to Twitter data can be a significant challenge. These data are owned by a private company that restricts access largely to protect the privacy of their subscribers. For example, Twitter removes users who decide to close their accounts, but Twitter has no way to make sure that these data have also been removed from all the copies made via the Twitter API. These restrictions have raised concerns about reproducibility of results, corporate influence, and stratification in the research community between a small elite that is well connected to social media companies and everyone else (Boyd & Crawford 2011; Huberman, 2012). New protocols and institutional arrangements are needed to align the goals and needs of industry and the academic community. In addition, advanced programming and other technical skills are required to access and process large semistructured datasets such as Twitter.

Measurement Issues

Although advances in identifying sentiment and opinion from text are proceeding rapidly (Pang & Lee 2008), we can only measure inner states indirectly, through their behavioral expression. For example, psychological lexicons (Pennebaker, Francis, & Booth, 2001) can be used to measure the expression of affective rhythms on Twitter on a global scale (Golder & Macy, 2011), but these methods cannot account for temporal lags between expression and experience.

An important limitation in all observational studies of network contagion, whether online or offline, is the difficulty distinguishing between homophily and contagion. Homophily refers to a variety of selection mechanisms by which a social tie is more likely between individuals with similar attributes and environmental exposures (McPherson, Smith-Lovin, & Cook, 2001). Contagion refers to influence mechanisms (e.g., imitation or peer pressure) by which traits diffuse along network edges. Homophily and contagion offer competing explanations for network autocorrelation, which refers to the greater similarity in the attributes of closely connected nodes. Based on simulated networks, Shalizi and Thomas (2011) conclude that "there is just no way to separate selection from influence observationally" (see also Manski, 1993). This does not mean that observational studies using online networks are useless, but researchers need to refrain from assuming that the observed network autocorrelation reflects contagion effects and to acknowledge that the similarity between adjacent nodes may reflect the mutually reinforcing effects of influence and selection whose separate contributions may be impossible to tease apart. For example, although Ugander et al. (2012) controlled for demographic similarity (sex, age, and nationality), there are countless other ways in which shared environments, affiliations, interests, and personality traits might cause two friends to join Facebook independently but not on the same day, making it look like the "early adopter" influenced the friend they invited who would have joined anyway.

One solution is to conduct controlled experiments that manipulate exposure to a possible contagion, as in the Facebook experiment by Bond et al. (2012). Where experimental methods are not feasible and the only data are observational, researchers can tease apart influence and selection by using an instrumental variable that is correlated with actors' neighbors' exposure to the contagion but not to actors' own exposure and then comparing the presence of the contagion among actors with and without exposed neighbors (Imbens & Angrist, 1994).

Another fundamental problem in online as well as offline network studies is deciding what constitutes a social tie (Butts, 2009). In survey-based research on ego networks, controversy has centered on how to ask respondents to nominate a friend. In studies using Twitter messages, a key question is how to determine the type and number of exchanges that are necessary to indicate the existence of an enduring social relationship (Borgatti & Halgin, 2011). For example, researchers need to decide whether to use follower relations (in which two users each follow the other), "@mentions" in which two users refer or reply to each other (Honeycutt & Herring, 2009), or retweets in which two users each repost what the other has written (Boyd, Golder, & Lotan, 2010; Conover et al., 2011). A related issue is whether the metric for establishing a link is consonant with the actors' conception of a social relationship. These questions arise as well in studies of offline networks, particularly affiliation networks, for which a number of heuristics have been proposed to determine whether the edge corresponds to an actual interaction, such as similarity (Flynn, Reagans, & Guillory, 2010), regularity of structure and kinship terms (Brashears, 2013), and indications of instrumental versus sentimental ties (Freeman, 1992). One study of Twitter networks confirmed that follower relations do not correspond to offline friendships. However, they developed new algorithms that detect offline friendships using a novel measure of user closeness (Xie et al., 2012).

A similar issue arises in deciding where to set the threshold for which users to include in the analysis, given that active participation in online environments is often highly skewed (Preece & Shneiderman, 2009). Low-activity users may not represent committed members, but arbitrary thresholds may also have the effect of artificially excluding a large number, even a majority, of individuals from the analysis, with potentially misleading effects on network measures such as density, degree distribution, and mean path length.

Tufekci (2014) calls attention to several additional methodological challenges posed by data obtained from Twitter. These include the validity and representativeness of conclusions derived from a single platform, sampling biases arising from selection by hashtags, vague and unrepresentative sampling frames, and field effects (e.g., diffusion of content outside the Twitter network).

Is the Online World a Parallel Universe?

Researchers also face the challenge of generalizing from online to offline behavior. Interactions offline differ in important and obvious ways from those online, including the lifting of geographic and temporal constraints on face-to-face communication. For example, the ability to wait to respond to an @mention affords the opportunity to be introspective and more deliberate and strategic about one's self-presentation (Goffman, 1959). The anonymity permitted by Twitter frees users to invent an entirely new persona, raising doubts about the credibility of demographic profile data. Anonymity can also permit or encourage the production of the vitriolic speech that pervades many online conversations but is generally unthinkable offline. Differences between online and offline modes of communication have been the subject of a number of studies focusing on their comparative "richness," or the bandwidth available for the transmission of verbal and visual cues (Daft & Lengel, 1986; Walther, 2007). Although face-to-face interaction is richer visually, there are other aspects of online communication that can be much denser than their offline counterparts, such as the ready availability of persistent histories (Hollan & Stornetta, 1992) and the opportunity to craft novel modes of expression, such as the emoticon or Twitter "@reply" (Herring, 1999; Menchik & Tian 2008; Honeycutt & Herring 2009).

Early studies also raised questions about possible distorting effects of online access. The "displacement" theory posited that Internet use was an asocial activity that took time away from family and friends (Nie & Hillygus, 2002), and empirical research showed that these effects varied, depending on the type of online activity (Kraut & Kiesler, 2003). However, this research predates the "social media" era, and more recent research (Robinson, 2011a) suggests that the displacement theory is less relevant today.

The "digital divide" raises additional concerns about generalizing from the online to offline populations. The Twitter population tends to be younger, better educated, and more affluent, which also raises important questions about the potential for reproducing and even amplifying social stratification. Even where the technological access is available, the skills to make use of that access remain unevenly distributed (DiMaggio et al., 2001; Hargittai 2010; Robinson 2011b), likely leading to biased levels of participation. Nevertheless, these differences do not warrant the widely used distinction between Twitter and the "real world," with the implication that Twitter users enter a metaphysical realm every time they access their account. The Twitter world is not identical to the offline world, but it is entirely real. Users who desire status, admiration, social approval, and attention in their offline relationships will bring those desires with them to Twitter. Individuals must navigate many of the same social obstacles online as they do offline as they seek information, political support, friendship, romance, or consumer goods.

While the activities and populations differ from the offline counterparts, the differences are rapidly declining as Twitter grows globally and online interactions are becoming more fully integrated with people's daily offline activities. As the number of users increases, Twitter has the potential to become the primary mechanism by which people engage in many everyday activities, such as following the news; arguing about politics, sports, music, and movies; maintaining social ties with friends and family; shopping; dating; and even seeking employment. An early study (Wellman & Hampton, 1999) found online and offline networks were already merging as early as the 1990s, as neighborhoods and local communities began to use electronic communication tools to augment their existing modes of communication. With the growing use of mobile technologies, Twitter provides an increasingly seamless transition between the offline and online worlds (Rainie & Wellman, 2012, Xie et al., 2012). Even though users have the ability to remain pseudonymous, they often establish longstanding and cherished identities and reputations that they are reluctant to cast off.

Though Twitter may differ fundamentally in the demographic profile of its users, not only from the offline world but even from other online communities, these differences can also open up research possibilities. Just as offline social clubs, community groups, street gangs, firms, and specialized organizations can be opportunities for comparative case studies, so too can highly idiosyncratic online communities, such as Couchsurfing and a local message board, that differ from Twitter in theoretically important ways.

In sum, online interaction is already deeply woven into the daily experience of millions of people worldwide, and the number of Twitter users is rapidly growing. Though differential levels of access, skills, and engagement persist, those differences are declining as usage becomes increasingly universal. For millions, socializing, dating, shopping, and learning take place in a digital environment that is second nature.

Methods, Skills, and Training

A primarily obstacle to online research by social scientists is the need for advanced technical training to collect, store, manipulate, analyze, and validate massive quantities of semistructured data, such as text generated by hundreds of millions of social media users. In addition, advanced programming skills are required to interact with specialized or custom hardware, to execute tasks in parallel on computing grids composed of hundreds of nodes that span the globe, and simply to ensure that very large amounts of data consume memory efficiently and are processed using algorithms that run in a reasonable amount of time. As a consequence, the first wave of studies of online behavior and interaction has been dominated by physical, computer, and information scientists who may lack the theoretical grounding necessary to know where to look, what questions to ask, or what the results may imply. In the short term, multidisciplinary collaborations can be highly fruitful, but the long-run solution is for graduate programs in the social sciences to adapt to the era of "big data" by providing training in skills that are needed for online research. The list includes:

- Making use of programming interfaces. Many commercial services, in the interest of interoperating with other services as well as third-party software developers, provide APIs that make it possible to download data from the service in a structured and permissible way. In order to use an API, the researcher must typically first register for an "API key" or unique access token and then write a script to successively query the service and retrieve the desired information. Chapter 1 of this volume discusses how the Twitter API can be used to conduct social science research, outlining key challenges and strategies for collecting datasets that track a particular crisis or event.

- Manipulating unstructured data and nested data structures. Data retrieved via APIs are often structured very differently from the flat files that social scientists are trained to work with. Online data are likely to have nested structures, as in XML or JSON documents, that cannot be directly imported into standard statistical packages. Learning to use regular expressions makes it much easier to transform data from human-readable to machine-readable format.

- Manipulating and storing large datasets. Finding the degree distribution or average path length in a social network with hundreds of millions of individuals, or the relative frequency of positive and negative emotion words in a large text corpus (Golder & Macy, 2011), could be impractical or impossible on a single computer. However, the problem of computational load can be addressed by parallelizing the task on a computer cluster. Among the most important innovations in computing in the past decade has been the development of the MapReduce programming paradigm (Dean & Ghemawat, 2004) and the availability of commodity cloud storage. Developed at Google to process the petabytes of web pages the search engine collects, MapReduce provides a convenient way to work with data that are too large to process (or even fit) on a single computer. A series of transformations are performed in succession on subsets of a large dataset, each of which resides on a different computer or processing node. Following these transformations, aggregations are performed so that summary statistics may be generated. Storing large datasets has similarly been made easier, due to the availability of commodity cloud storage. For example, Amazon.com's Web Services and Microsoft's Azure[4] platform rent Internet-based computing resources, such as servers that can be used for pennies per hour or storage that costs pennies per gigabyte. Researchers faced with spending thousands of dollars of research funds on computer hardware may find this to be a cost-effective alternative, since there is no upfront cost, resources may be turned off when no longer needed, and information technology (IT) staff do not need to be hired to support or manage the equipment.

- Machine learning, sentiment analysis, and topic modeling. Machine learning refers to statistical techniques that use past observations to classify new observations or make predictions about the associated outcomes. These techniques may be useful when data have nonlinear relationships or a large number of variables that interact in a complex system in ways that cannot be modeled by traditional regression-based methods. Applications range from understanding natural human language to detecting which emails are spam. For example, Support Vector Machines and decision trees make it possible for researchers to code only a random sample from a massive set of observations and approximate the rest. Text analysis techniques such as Latent Dirichlet Allocation (LDA) perform unsupervised topic modeling or automatic clustering of the words found in a body of texts into topical groups (Blei, Ng, & Jordan, 2003) by examining the co-occurrences of the words found within. Sentiment analysis uses a combination of statistical techniques and human-created lexicons to identify the valence and intensity of various emotional states expressed in a body of text. Libraries that perform some of these techniques are available in R, or in stand-alone software packages such as University of Waikato's Weka[5] or Stanford's Topic Modeling Toolbox.[6]

One reason these methods have not gained greater currency in the social sciences is that many current applications are deliberately atheoretical, placing higher value on the ability to predict future observations than on testing a theoretically motivated hypothesis. However, one should not throw out the methodological baby with the atheoretical bathwater. After all, every research method, from linear regression to participant observation, can be applied descriptively, with little or no theoretical direction, or analytically,

[4] See http://aws.amazon.com and http://windowsazure.com, respectively.
[5] http://www.cs.waikato.ac.nz/ml/weka/.
[6] http://nlp.stanford.edu/software/tmt/tmt-0.4/.

in a program of research that targets the underlying causal mechanisms. Twitter data open up transformative possibilities for both descriptive and analytical studies, but without the automated data management and coding tools developed by computer scientists, the analysis of massive unstructured data will remain beyond the reach of most social scientists, leaving the field to disciplines that are much better at building powerful telescopes than at knowing where to point them (Lazer et al., 2009; Watts, 2012). Although few social science departments are currently able to incorporate these skills into graduate methods courses, interested students can be directed to computer and information science departments for specialized training. Many of these methodological and analytical challenges are addressed in the chapters that follow, in particular Chapter 1.

Conclusion

In the earliest days of the field of information theory, Claude Shannon's (1956) "The Bandwagon" essay warned that the flurry of interest in the new field would generate a large amount of low-quality work, but this should not lead the research community to conclude that this was an inherent limitation. On the contrary, it should be taken as an exhortation to focus on producing more rigorous studies. Shannon's advice may apply as well to the coming era of online social science. The unprecedented opportunity to observe human behavior and social interaction in real time, at a microscopic level yet on a global scale, is attracting widespread interest among scientists with the requisite skills to mine these data but not always with the theoretical background needed to guide the inquiry. Studies that identify patterns of behavior or map social landscapes invite dismissal as "atheoretic empiricism," but this may be shortsighted. These pioneering studies should instead be taken as evidence not of the most that can be learned using data from Twitter, but of the vast opportunities that lie ahead for a new science of social life.

References

Backstrom, L., Dwork, C., and Kleinberg, J. 2007. Wherefore art thou r3579x? Anonymized social networks, hidden patterns, and structural steganography. In *Proceedings of the 16th International Conference on the World Wide Web* (pp. 181–90). ACM.

Backstrom, L., and Kleinberg, J. 2014. Romantic partnerships and the dispersion of social ties: a network analysis of relationship status on Facebook. In *Proceedings of the 17th ACM Conference on Computer Supported Cooperative Work & Social Computing* (pp. 831–41). ACM.

Blei, D. M., Ng, A. Y., and Jordan, M. I. 2003. Latent dirichlet allocation. *Journal of Machine Learning Research*, 3, 993.

Bond, R. M., Fariss, C. J., Jones, J. J., Kramer, A. D. I., Marlow, C., et al. 2012. A 61-million-person experiment in social influence and political mobilization. *Nature*, 489(7415), 295.

Borgatti, S. P., and Halgin, D. S. 2011. On network theory. *Organization Science*, 22, 1168–81.

Boutyline, A., and Willer, R. 2011. The social structure of political echo chambers: ideology leads to asymmetries in online political communication networks. Working paper, University of California Berkeley.

boyd, D., and Crawford, K. 2011. Six provocations for big data. Paper presented at Oxford Internet Institute's "A Decade in Internet Time: Symposium on the Dynamics of the Internet and Society."

boyd, D., Golder, S. A., and Lotan, G. 2010. Tweet, tweet, retweet: conversational aspects of retweeting on Twitter. In *Proceedings of the 43rd Hawaii International Conference on System Sciences (HICSS-43)* (pp. 1–10). IEEE.

Brashears, M. E. 2013. Humans use compression heuristics to improve the recall of social networks. *Nature Scientific Reports*, 1513(3), 1513.

Burt, R. S. 1997. A note on social capital and network content. *Social Networks*, 19, 355.

Butts, C. T. 2009. Revisiting the foundations of network analysis. *Science*, 325, 414.

Centola, D. 2010. The spread of behavior in an online social network experiment. *Science*, 329, 1194.

Centola, D., and Macy, M. 2007. Complex contagions and the weakness of long ties. *American Journal of Sociology*, 113(3), 702.

Cha, M., Haddadi, H., Benevenuto, F., and Gummadi, K. P. 2010. Measuring user influence in Twitter: the million follower fallacy. In *Proceedings of the 4th International AAAI Conference on Weblogs and Social Media* (pp. 10–17). AAAI.

Compton, R., Jurgens, D., Allen, D., "Geotagging One Hundred Million Twitter Accounts with Total Variation Minimization." arXiv:1404.7152, 4 Mar 2015. DOI: 10.1109/BigData.2014.7004256.

Conover, M. D., Ratkiewicz, J., Francisco, M., Gonc, B., Flammini, A., and Menczer, F. 2011. Political polarization on Twitter. Working paper, Center for Complex Networks and Systems Research.

Daft, R. L., and Lengel, R. H. 1986. Organizational information requirements, media richness and structural design. *Management Science*, 32(5), 554.

De Montjoye, Y-A., Hidalgo, C. A., Verleysen, M., and Blondel, V. D. 2013. Unique in the crowd: the privacy bounds of human mobility. *Scientific Reports*, 3, 1376.

Dean, J., and Ghemawat, S. 2004. MapReduce: simplified data processing on large clusters. In *Proceedings of OSDI'04: 6th Conference on Symposium on Operating System Design Implementation (OSDI'04)* (pp. 137–49). USENIX Association.

Della Posta, D., Shi, Y., and Macy, M. W. 2013. Why do liberals drink lattes? Working paper, Cornell University Social Dynamics Laboratory.

Digrazia, J., McKelvey, K., Bollen, J., and Rojas, F. 2013. More tweets, more votes: social media as a quantitative indicator of political behavior. *PLOS ONE*, 8:e70449.

DiMaggio, P., Hargittai, E., Neuman, W. R., and Robinson, J. P. 2001. Social implications of the Internet. *Annual Review of Sociology*, 27, 307.

Duncan, O. D. 1966. Path analysis: sociological examples. *American Journal of Sociology*, 72(1), 1.

Entwisle, B., Faust, K., Rindfuss, R. R., and Kaneda, T. 2007. Networks and contexts: variation in the structure of social ties. *American Journal of Sociology*, 112(5), 1495.

Fischer, C. S. 2009. The 2004 GSS finding of shrunken social networks: an artifact? *American Sociological Review*, 74(4), 657.

Flynn, F. J., Reagans, R. E., and Guillory, L. 2010. Do you two know each other? Transitivity, homophily and the need for (network) closure. *Journal of Personality and Social Psychology*, 99(5), 855.

Freeman, L. C. 1992. Filling in the blanks: a theory of cognitive categories and the structure of social affiliation. *Social Psychology Quarterly*, 55(2), 118.

Gayo-Avello, D. 2012. No, you cannot predict elections with Twitter. *IEEE Internet Computing*, 16(6), 91.

Gladwell, M. 2000. *The Tipping Point: How Little Things Can Make a Big Difference*. Little, Brown.

Goffman, E. 1959. *The Presentation of Self in Everyday Life*. Anchor.

Golder, S. A, and Macy, M. W. 2011. Diurnal and seasonal mood vary with work, sleep and daylength across diverse cultures. *Science*, 333, 1878.

Golder, S. A., and Yardi, S. 2010. Structural predictors of tie formation in Twitter: transitivity and mutuality. In *Proceedings of the 2nd IEEE International Conference on Social Computing* (pp. 88–95). IEEE.

González-Bailón, S., Borge-Holthoefer, J., Rivero, A., and Moreno, Y. 2011. The dynamics of protest recruitment through an online network. *Scientific Reports*, 1, 1.

Hargittai, E. 2010. Digital na(t)ives? Variation in Internet skills and uses among members of the net generation. *Sociological Inquiry*, 80(1), 92.

Harris, K. M., Halpern, C. T., Whitsel, E., Hussey, J., Tabor, J., and Entzel, P. 2009. *The National Longitudinal Study of Adolescent Health: Research Design*.

Herring, S. C. 1999. Interactional coherence in CMC. *Journal of Computer-Mediated Communication*, 4(4).

Hollan, J., and Stornetta, S. 1992. Beyond being there. In *Proceedings of the SIGCHI Conference on Human Factors in Computing Systems – CHI '92* (pp. 119–25). ACM.

Honeycutt, C., and Herring, S. C. 2009. Beyond microblogging: conversation and collaboration via Twitter. In *Proceedings of the 42nd Hawaii International Conference on Systems Science* (pp. 1–10). IEEE.

Huberman, B. A. 2012. Big data deserve a bigger audience. *Nature*, 482, 308.

Imbens, G. W, and Angrist, J. D. 1994. Identification and estimation of local average treatment effects. *Econometrica*, 62(2), 467.

Jernigan, C., and Mistree, B. F. T. 2009. Gaydar: Facebook friendships expose sexual orientation. *First Monday*, 14(10).

Katz, E., and Lazarsfeld, P. 1955. *Personal Influence*. Free Press.

Kraut, R., and Kiesler, S. 2003. The social impact of Internet use. *Psychological Science Agenda*, summer, 8–10.

Kuhn, T. 1962. *The Structure of Scientific Revolutions*, 3rd ed. University of Chicago Press.

Kwak, H., Lee, C., Park, H., and Moon, S. 2010. What is Twitter, a social network or a news media? In *Proceedings of the 19th International Conference on World Wide Web* (pp. 519–600). ACM.

Lazer, D., Pentland, A., Adamic, L., Aral, S., Barabási, A-L., et al. 2009. Computational social science. *Science*, 323, 721.

Lovelace, R. V. E., and Tyler, G. L. 2012. On the discovery of the period of the crab nebula pulsar. *Observatory*, 132(3), 186.

Lyman, P., and Wakeford N. 1999. Going into the (virtual) field. *American Behavioral Scientist*, 43(3), 359.

Macy, M. W, and Willer, R. 2002. From factors to actors: computational sociology and agent-based modeling. *Annual Review of Sociology*, 28(1), 143.

Manski, C. F. 1993. Identification of endogenous social effects: the reflection problem. *Review of Economic Studies*, 60(3), 531.

Marsden, P. V. 1990. Network data and measurement. *Annual Review of Sociology*, 16, 435.

McPherson, M. 2004. A blau space primer: prolegomenon to an ecology of affiliation. *Industrial and Corporate Change*, 13(1), 263.

McPherson, M., Smith-Lovin, L., and Cook, J. M. 2001. Birds of a feather: homophily in social networks. *Annual Review of Sociology*, 27, 415.

Menchik, D. A., and Tian, X. 2008. Putting social context into text: the semiotics of e-mail interaction. *American Journal of Sociology*, 114(2), 332.

Nie, N. H., and Hillygus, D. S. 2002. The impact of Internet use on sociability: time-diary findings. *IT & Society*, 1(1), 1.

Paccagnella, L. 1997. Getting the seats of your pants dirty: strategies for ethnographic research on virtual communities. *Journal of Computer-Mediated Communication*, 3(1).

Pang, B., and Lee, L. 2008. Opinion mining and sentiment analysis. *Foundations and Trends in Information Retrieval*, 2(1–2), 1.

Pennebaker, J. W., Francis, M. E., and Booth, R. J. 2001. *Linguistic Inquiry and Word Count (LIWC): LIWC2001*. Lawrence Erlbaum Associates.

Pinch, T. J., and Bijker, W. E. 1984. The social construction of facts and artefacts: or how the sociology of science and the sociology of technology might benefit each other. *Social Studies of Science*, 14(3), 399.

Podolny, J. M. 2001. Networks as pipes and prisms of the market. *American Journal of Sociology*, 107(1), 33.

Preece, J., and Shneiderman, B. 2009. The reader-to-leader framework: motivating technology-mediated social participation. *AIS Transactions on Human-Computer Interaction*, 1(1), 13.

Pustejovsky, J. E., and Spillane, J. P. 2009. Question-order effects in social network name generators. *Social Networks*, 31(4), 221.

Rainie, L., and Wellman, B. 2012. *Networked: The New Social Operating System*. MIT Press

Robinson, J. P. 2011a. IT use and leisure time displacement. *Information, Communication and Society*, 14(4), 495.

Robinson, L. 2011b. Information channel preferences and information opportunity structures. *Information, Communication and Society*, 14(4), 472.

Romero, D. M., Meeder, B., and Kleinberg, J. 2011. Differences in the mechanics of information diffusion across topics: idioms, political hashtags, and complex contagion on Twitter. In *Proceedings of the 20th International Conference on World Wide Web (WWW2011)* (pp. 695–704). ACM.

Salganik, M. J., Dodds, P. S., and Watts, D. J. 2006. Experimental study of inequality and unpredictability in an artificial cultural market. *Science*, 311, 854.

Shalizi, C. R., and Thomas, A. C. 2011. Homophily and contagion are generically confounded in observational social network studies. *Sociolocal Methods and Research*, 40(2), 211.

Shannon, C. 1956. The bandwagon. *IRE Transactions on Information Theory*, 2 (1), 3.

State, B., Abrahao, B., and Cook, K. 2012. From power to status in large scale online exchanges. In *Proceedings of the 4th ACM Conference on Web Science (WebSci)* (http.websci2.org). ACM.

Sunstein, C. R. 2001. *Republic.com*. Princeton University Press.

Tufekci, Z. 2014. Big questions for social media big data: representativeness, validity and other methodological pitfalls. In *Eighth International AAAI Conference on Weblogs and Social Media*. http://arxiv.org/ftp/arxiv/papers/1403/1403.7400.pdf.

Ugander, J., Backstrom, L., Marlow, C., and Kleinberg, J. 2012. Structural diversity in social contagion. *Proceedings of the National Academy of Sciences of the United States of America*, 109(16), 5962.

Walther, J. B. 2007. Selective self-presentation in computer-mediated communication: hyperpersonal dimensions of technology, language, and cognition. *Computers in Human Behavior*, 23, 2538.

Watts, D. J. 2012. *Everything Is Obvious: How Common Sense Fails Us*. Crown Business.

Weber, I., Garimella, V., and Batayneh, A. 2013. Secular vs Islamist polarization in Egypt on Twitter. In *Proceedings of the 2013 IEEE/ACM International Conference on Advances in Social Networks Analysis and Mining* (pp. 290–7). ACM.

Weber, M. 1922. *Economy and Society*. University of California Press.

Wellman, B., and Hampton, K. 1999. Living networked on and offline. *Contemporary Sociology*, 28(6), 648.

Weng, L., Menczer, F., and Ahn, Y-Y. 2013. Virality prediction and community structure in social networks. *Scientific Reports*, 3: 2522.

Wright, S. 1934. The method of path coefficients. *Annals of Mathematical Statistics*, 5(3), 161.

Xie, W., Li, C., Zhu, F., Lim, E-P., and Gong, X. 2012. When a friend in Twitter is a friend in life. In *Proceedings of the 3rd Annual ACM Web Science Conference on – WebSci '12* (pp. 344–7). ACM.

Yardi, S., Romero, D. M., Schoenebeck, G., and Boyd, D. 2010. Detecting spam in a Twitter network. *First Monday*, 15(1).

Zachary, W. W. 1977. An information flow model for conflict and fission in small groups. *Journal of Anthropological Research*, 33, 452.

Zizzo, D. J. 2010. Experimenter demand effects in economic experiments. *Experimental Economics*, 13(1),75.

1

Analyzing Twitter Data

Shamanth Kumar, Fred Morstatter, and Huan Liu

Twitter is a social network with over 250 million active users who collectively generate more than 500 million tweets each day. In social sciences research, Twitter has earned the focus of extensive research largely due to its openness in sharing its public data. Twitter exposes an extensive application programming interfaces (APIs) that can be used to collect a wealth of social data. In this chapter, we introduce these APIs and discuss how they can be used to conduct social sciences research. We also outline some issues that arise when using these APIs, and some strategies for collecting datasets that can give insight into a particular event.

1. Introduction

Twitter is a rich data source that provides several forms of information generated through the interaction of its users. These data can be harnessed to accomplish a variety of personalization and prediction tasks. Recently, Twitter data have been used to predict things as diverse as election results (Tumasjan et al., 2010; c.f. Chapter 2) or the location of earthquakes (Sakaki et al., 2010; c.f. Chapter 6). Twitter currently has over 250 million active users who collectively generate more than 500 million tweets each day.[1] This creates a unique opportunity to conduct large-scale studies on user behavior. An important step before conducting such studies is the identification and collection of data relevant to the problem.

Twitter is an online social networking platform where the registered users can create connections and share messages with other users. Messaging on

---

[1] http://mashable.com/2014/04/29/twitter-q1-earnings-2014/.

Twitter is unique, as messages are required to be at most 140 characters long, and these messages are normally broadcast to all the users on Twitter. Thus, the platform provides an avenue to share content with a large and diverse population with few resources. These interactions generate different kinds of information. Information is made accessible to the public via APIs or interfaces where requests for data can be submitted. In this chapter, we introduce different forms of Twitter data and illustrate the capabilities and restrictions imposed by the API on Twitter data analysis. We will also describe methods to process and enrich data to facilitate its analysis. Finally, we will present examples of research issues that have been investigated using Twitter data.

The first task in working with Twitter data is collecting the information necessary for the study. But, before we discuss how this can be accomplished, we introduce some fundamental information about the overall process of collecting Twitter data.

1.1. *Twitter API Types*

Twitter provides two forms of public APIs to access Twitter data geared toward different use cases. APIs can be used to collect historic information, such as the tweets published by a user in the past and the social connections of a user. The streaming APIs provide uninterrupted access to real-time information, such as the public tweets of a user as they are generated. Detailed documentation on the APIs can be found at the Twitter developer's website.[2] The two forms of Twitter API provide access to information at different scales and can be used in conjunction to accomplish the analysis of information on Twitter. Twitter APIs can be accessed only through registered Twitter applications.

Both forms of the Twitter API can be accessed using the following general procedure:

1. Authenticate to Twitter using the Open Authentication (OAuth) mechanism.
2. Create a call to a Twitter API with suitable parameters.
3. Receive and process the response from the API.

Both types of API, along with the data they return, can be tested online through a console provided by Apigee.[3]

---

[2]   http://dev.twitter.com.
[3]   https://apigee.com/console/twitter.

1.1.1. Twitter Applications

Twitter APIs are accessible only via applications registered on Twitter. To access the Twitter APIs, one must register an application on the Twitter developer's website to indicate the intended use of Twitter data.[4] Upon registering an application, two application-specific keys are generated. These keys are called consumer key and consumer secret. The two keys are required in the authentication process and serve to identify the application to Twitter. Requests to Twitter APIs also require an access token and secret, which are generated when a Twitter user authorizes an application to access Twitter on his or her behalf. These four identifiers must be provided in all requests to the API and are used to decide the number of requests from an application that will be honored by the APIs.

1.1.2. Open Authentication

Open Authentication is an open standard for authentication that has been adopted by Twitter to provide access to protected information. OAuth was designed with the intention of creating an authentication protocol that was easy, secure, and open, as passwords are highly vulnerable to theft. Using Open Authentication, Twitter applications can authenticate users without requiring access to their Twitter credentials. A more detailed discussion on Open Authentication can be found in Kumar, Morstatter, and Liu (2014a).

Next, we discuss the forms of data generated on Twitter and introduce the APIs that can be used to access them.

2. Aggregating Twitter Data

Examples of data generated on Twitter include short messages, content generated as a result of the network interactions between users, other user activity such as updating profiles, and descriptive information about a user's interests. The availability of Twitter data via flexible APIs make Twitter an attractive platform to access a large volume of user-generated information and to conduct studies on user behavior in social media. Here, we discuss in greater detail what data are available and how they can be aggregated.

2.1. *Forms of Twitter Data*

2.1.1. Content

Typically, the messages generated on Twitter are considered public unless the publishing user explicitly declares them private. Public tweets are visible to

---

[4] New applications can be registered at https://apps.twitter.com/app/new.

any registered user on Twitter, and even to nonregistered users who access a user's Twitter profile through a web browser. However, this behavior can be limited via privacy settings. Registered users can also choose to "follow" other users and be provided with an aggregated feed of all those users' tweets. We discuss "following" in more detail later.

There are two special forms of Tweets:

- Directed tweets[5]: Ordinarily, messages are broadcast to all the followers of a user. A directed message can be sent to a specific user by beginning the tweet with the intended recipient's username. For example, consider the following tweet sent from "Bob" to "Greg": "@Greg welcome to Twitter." Here the message is directly sent to "Greg" and is, by default, not sent to other followers of "Bob."[6]
- Retweets: Messages originally posted by other users can be reposted to one's followers as a retweet. These messages are characterized by the "RT @username" pattern at the beginning of the tweet, where the username points to the original author of the tweet's content. Following is an example of a retweet published by the user "Bob": "RT @Jim: What an interesting tweet!" Retweets are part of the message propagation mechanism on Twitter. Typically, messages with a large number of retweets are considered interesting.

While directed messages are conversations occurring between users, retweets represent the propagation of information through Twitter's social network and can be used to investigate epidemiological questions. Twitter messages can also contain artifacts, such as a hashtag or a uniform resource locator (URL). A hashtag is a word preceded by the sign #, and they are used to indicate the topic of a tweet.

URLs are typically shortened by Twitter to accommodate the character restriction on the message length. Expanding the content of the tweet via the information contained in the external URLs can be challenging due to this policy. However, there exist services, such as the LongURL API,[7] that can be used to expand the shortened links with ease. Additionally, the "entities" field of the Twitter object can be used to obtain the expanded URL. We discuss strategies to expand URLs in Section 3.1.3.

---

[5] These usually public tweets are not to be confused with "Direct Messages," which are always private, are not visible to other users, and can only be sent to followers, that is, other Twitter users who have explicitly expressed interest in a user's updates.

[6] See https://blog.twitter.com/2012/a-new-way-to-experience-profiles-with-or-without-replies for the reasons behind this separate treatment.

[7] http://longurl.org/.

Curated Tweets: The large volume of tweets can be overwhelming and often noisy when used in studies to infer user attributes. For this reason, tweets can be curated, which enables them to be used to fetch more focused tweets. There are two ways in which Twitter allows tweets to be curated:

• **Favorite tweets:** Twitter users can recognize interesting tweets and save them for later reading through the "favorite" mechanism. Tweets marked as "favorite" are saved in a user's profile for viewing later and can be accessed efficiently from Twitter's interface. The user can fetch these tets using Twitter's REST APIs to retrieve a more focused view of the user's interests.

• **Lists:** Curation of tweets can also be accomplished at the user level by creating "lists" of users. Often such lists include users who publish content on similar topics, such as the list of accounts posting Hurricane Sandy–related information created by BBC News.[8]

API and Limitations: A user's tweets can be collected using the /statuses/user_timeline[9] REST API. At the time of this writing, one can retrieve 3,200 of the most recent tweets published by a user, including retweets. A continuous stream of recent tweets can also be accessed using the streaming API. Returned tweets also typically contain the publishing user's information, as discussed later.

2.1.2. Social Networks

Twitter users actively connect with other users to gain access to their content. This behavior, called "following," is Twitter's mechanism to create social networks. Therefore, Twitter is a directed network with two types of connections between users. A user can choose to follow other users and can also be followed by other users for their content. In Figure 1.1, we can observe an example of such connections. "John" follows "Alice," therefore "John" is "Alice's" follower. "Alice" follows "Peter," therefore "Peter," in Twitter terminology, is a friend of "Alice." To follow another user, a user simply initiates this relationship. Only in the case of protected users, who have chosen more conservative privacy settings, all followers need to be approved by the user before the relationship is finalized. Twitter's social network has found a variety of network-based solutions to problems such as sentiment analysis (Hu et al., 2013a) and user location prediction (Rout et al., 2013).

API and Limitations: The followers of a user can be crawled from Twitter using the API followers/list.[10] The response from Twitter consists of an array

---

[8] https://twitter.com/BBCNewsUS/lists/hurricane-sandy.
[9] https://dev.twitter.com/docs/api/1.1/get/statuses/user_timeline.
[10] https://dev.twitter.com/docs/api/1.1/get/followers/list.

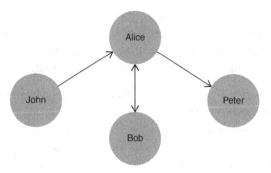

Figure 1.1. An example of a Twitter social network with follower and following relationships.

of user profiles. At the time of this writing, at most fifteen API calls from a user and thirty API calls per application are allowed within a rate limit window, which currently spans 15 minutes.[11] The friends of a user can similarly be crawled using the Twitter API friends/list,[12] restricted by the same rate limits. A user's network is only accessible using the REST API, and at the time of this writing the streaming APIs cannot be used to fetch this information.

2.1.3. User Profiles

Twitter users describe themselves to other users through their Twitter profiles. A user's profile can be a rich source of information about the user. A Twitter profile typically consists of the following distinct pieces of information about the user:

- User's real name: a free text field where the user can choose to enter his or her real name. While this is the encouraged practice, no check is made to ensure that this is the user's real name. (However, the authenticity of the information cannot be verified.)
- User's Twitter handle: the user's official Twitter username.
- Twitter ID: a unique numeric ID assigned by Twitter to a user at the time of registration.
- User's location: a free text field where the user can contribute his or her location.
- URL: a web address that typically points to a more detailed profile of the user on an external website, such as a public blog or Facebook page.
- A textual description of the user and his or her interests.

---

[11] https://dev.twitter.com/docs/rate-limiting/1.1.
[12] https://dev.twitter.com/docs/api/1.1/get/friends/list.

- The number of friends and followers of the user.
- A count of all tweets published by the user.
- Verified mark: when a user's real identity has been determined by Twitter to be as portrayed by the user's profile on Twitter, the user is marked as verified. This is typically performed for public figures and celebrities.
- A link to the user's profile picture.
- The date and time the user created the account.

API and Limitations: A user's profile can be retrieved using the REST APIs (users/show).[13] The API accepts a valid username or a Twitter ID as a parameter. At the time of this writing, at most 180 API calls from a single application can be made within a single rate limit window of 15 minutes. A user's profile is also included as part of the metadata of a tweet, thus the publishing user's profile can be directly accessed when a Tweet is fetched. In addition to these methods of obtaining a user's profile, the profile information is also returned through every tweet received through the streaming API.

2.1.4. Searching Tweets

A very large volume of tweets is generated on Twitter every day. A flexible search provides the necessary tools to filter relevant information to conduct investigative studies. For example, consider a study on the political opinions of Twitter users in the United States. This would require us to have access to the tweets generated from within the country and therefore imply access to geographic information of the tweets. This can be accomplished on Twitter by searching for tweets generated from the geographic region spanned by the nation that provide the necessary geographic information. Content search on Twitter is facilitated through the use of such parameters. For example, to make the search more specific, one could also include terms that contain politically oriented words and phrases to the search. Acceptable parameter values for search include keywords, hashtags, phrases, geographic regions, usernames, or Twitter IDs. While the REST API provides access to a limited number of tweets, a continuous search can be accomplished using the streaming APIs.

API and Data Limitations: Both Streaming and REST APIs can be used to collect this information. The REST API (search/tweets)[14] at the time of this writing is limited to one hundred results per query. A distinguishing parameter for this API is the ability to search for tweets within a specific radius of a location, thus making it suitable for location-specific searches. The streaming APIs may be used to fetch future search results for geographic

---

[13] https://dev.twitter.com/docs/api/1.1/get/users/show.
[14] https://dev.twitter.com/docs/api/1.1/get/search/tweets.

regions described by rectangular boxes or keywords. The streaming APIs may be utilized in combination with the REST APIs to enhance the collection of tweets matching queries once interesting keywords and locations have been identified.

2.1.5. Data Response Format

Data collected from Twitter APIs and other tools are in the JavaScript Object Notation (JSON) format,[15] which is a popular data representation format for data on the web. JSON objects store data in the form of name/value pairs, the property names are unique and typically describe the property, and the value of the property corresponds to the value of the field. Information returned by the APIs is organized as an array of such objects, where each corresponds to one entity: a tweet or a user. An example of a tweet object can be observed in Listing 1.1, which presents a sample tweet. Here, the JSON object contains various properties that together describe a tweet, such as the "text" and the publishing user's "screen_name." Some fields are truncated or omitted in the example to improve readability. JSON parsing libraries are available for all major programming languages.[16] Online viewers such as JSONLint[17] can also be used to explore the structure of objects returned by Twitter APIs.

Listing 1.1 *An example of Twitter Tweet object.*

```
{
  "text": "This is the first Tweet.",
  "lang": "en",
  "id": 352914247774248960,
  "source": "web",
  "retweet_count": 0,
  "created_at": "Thu Jul 04 22:18:08 +0000 2013",
    // Other Tweet fields
  "place": {
    "place_type": "city",
    "name": "Tempe",
    "country_code": "US",
    "url": "https://api.twitter.com/1.1/geo/id/7
cb7440bcf83d464.json",
    "country": "United States",
    "full_name": "Tempe, AZ",
```

---

[15] http://www.json.org/.
[16] https://code.google.com/p/google-gson/.
[17] http://jsonlint.com/.

```
    // Other place fields
},
  " user ": {
  ... // User Information in the form of
Twitter user object
  }
}
```

3. Curating Twitter Data

In the previous section, we introduced the process through which Twitter data can be collected for research studies using the public APIs. In this section, we focus on how to prepare, process, store, and retrieve data effectively.

Data obtained through Twitter's APIs are generally well-formed. The APIs return JSON data wherein each field is documented, making it very easy to process these data for a researcher's own specific use. Even with this much structure, there are still some areas lacking form, where the meanings of the data and their interpretation are left up to interpretation. One of these areas is the content of the tweet, where people are free to enter any 140-character message they choose. How can we clean these data to make more sense of the text? Since Twitter is social media, there are many interactions that can be gleaned from this data, such as retweet networks, social networks, and more.

3.1. Enriching Twitter Data

3.1.1. Tokenization and Part of Speech Tagging

The text contained in tweets is often very different from standard English, or not in English at all. The text may contain misspellings, odd punctuation, non-English words, hashtags, emoticons, URLs, and more. Understanding this text is challenging, and preprocessing it for computational purposes can be tricky. One of the first steps in making sense out of tweets is to break the text up into smaller meaningful units, called tokens. Tokens can generally be thought of as words; however, they can also be other occurrences in the document, such as URLs and punctuation. Software systems that extract tokens from text are called tokenizers.

Another important action performed in cleaning the text is tagging each word with its part-of-speech (POS). POS analysis typically breaks down the terms of a sentence into categories such as verbs, nouns, and other classes. This, for example, allows to separate occurrences of "love" as a verb or noun, going beyond merely counting the word occurrences. Understanding the parts

Table 1.1. Output of the POS tagger from Owoputi et al. (2013) and the NER from Ritter et al. (2011) for a sample of tweets

Tweet Text	POS Tags	Named Entities
Props to Miguel	props/N to/P miguel/^	Miguel/person
Hey it's zombie time	hey/! it's/L zombie/A time/N	None
I will bet anyone who thinks Michigan is going to lose #champs	i/O will/V bet/V anyone/N who/O thinks/V michigan/ ^is/V going/V to/P lose/V #champs/#	Michigan/geo-loc

of speech employed by Twitter users can help provide critical insight into properties of the user. Automatic POS tagging has a long history; however, the challenge is escalated when it is applied to Twitter data. The ever-evolving language of Twitter users and the unpredictable grammatical structures used in tweets makes this a challenging problem.

One software tool that is tuned for Twitter data is the Twitter Natural Language Processing (NLP) and Part-of-Speech Tagger (Owoputi et al., 2013). This software performs both the tokenization and the POS tagging process, and it has been trained on Twitter data. By default, the tool uses a special tag set that is tuned for Twitter data. The tag set has special tags for Twitter-specific tokens such as hashtags and URLs, but also gives a coarser treatment to traditional tags such as nouns and verbs.[18] In this way, the software can perform these tasks with much higher accuracy than a standard off-the-shelf NLP package. Table 1.1 shows three example tweets run through this software. By employing these tools, we go from unstructured text to annotated, cleanly tokenized text that we can use in future processing.

3.1.2. Named Entity Recognition

Another important preprocessing task for Twitter text is named entity recognition (NER). NER tools find the nouns in the text of a document and categorize them into different predefined categories. Some examples of categories used by NER tools are businesses, places, times, and quantities. NER tools can help to make sense of Twitter data and can be used for many different aspects of social media. Examples include finding politicians mentioned in tweets to understand users' sentiment during campaigns, finding companies to

---

[18] A full list of ARK POS tags can be found in Owputi et al. (2013) and its implementation at http://www.ark.cs.cmu.edu/TweetNLP/.

measure consumer responses to a new product, or finding locations of protests in revolution-related data.

As with the tokenization and POS tagging task, the NER task is made extremely difficult by the unstructured and dynamic nature of Twitter text. Many of the named entities that will be tweeted in the future do not exist at the time of the building of the NER tool. Another issue is that one noun can refer to many possible entities: does a Tweet about "Chicago" reference a musical, a band, or a city? Despite this difficult challenge, the added benefit from having an understanding of the named entities in the text can give you depth in analyzing your data.

One named entity recognizer that has been built with Twitter data in mind can be found in Ritter et al. (2011). It attempts to organize the entities into ten categories that are commonly discussed on Twitter: person, geolocation, company, facility, product, band, sports team, movie, television show, and other. An example of some named entities extracted from tweets can be found in Table 1.1. Another example of a named entity recognition tool for Twitter is TwitIE (Bontcheva et al., 2013), which is accessible as an open source implementation.[19]

3.1.3. Recovering Shortened URLS

When a user posts a tweet to Twitter, all of the user's URLs are shortened to t.co to minimize the number of characters in the tweet. The problem introduced by URLs is that a shortened URL is specific both to the URL being shortened and to the user tweeting the shortened URL. This makes it difficult to study information propagation using these short URLs as it is no longer evident whether two users are tweeting the same URL or not. One strategy to get around this is to restore the original, long URL. In the JSON returned by Twitter, one can find the long URL in the "entities" field returned by the service.

3.1.4. Location Identification

Another important property of a tweet is the location from which it was published. In understanding the location, we can get a deeper sense of what the user's Tweet means, from whether the user is experiencing an event firsthand to extra information such as likely demographic properties of the user. Twitter's geotagging feature for its tweets provides incredibly accurate readings on the location of the tweet; by using the phone's Global Positioning System (GPS) sensor, the feature can locate the tweet often within one city block of the tweet's true location. The drawback of this approach is that Twitter users are

---

[19] http://gate.ac.uk/wiki/twitie.html.

Figure 1.2. An example of a Tweet with location information.

reluctant to share their location in their tweets, causing only about 1 percent of all of the tweets on Twitter to be geotagged (Morstatter et al. 2013b). The need for methods to identify a user's location is essential in situations such as a natural disaster, where such information may be used to obtain situational awareness or coordinate the response to a disaster. An example of a tweet message containing location information is shown in Figure 1.2.[20]

Location information on Twitter is available from two different sources:

- Geotagging information: Users can optionally choose to provide location information for the tweets they publish. This information can be highly accurate if the tweet was published using a smartphone with GPS capabilities.
- User profile: User location can be extracted from the location field in the user's profile. The information in the location field itself can be extracted using the aforementioned APIs.

An approach to finding geographic information for tweets that are not geotagged is to use the profile location of the user. Several web services take the profile location, a free-text field where the user can enter anything he or she pleases, and translate that into a location on the Earth in the form of a latitude/longitude point. Examples of location translation APIs include the

---

[20] https://twitter.com/nixs579/status/296093672691363842/photo/1.

Geonames API,[21] the open source Nominatim API from OpenStreetMaps,[22] and MapQuest.[23] Similar APIs are also provided by Bing,[24] Google,[25] and Yahoo! BOSS GeoServices.[26] However, they are generally more restrictive with respect to the number of requests. A weakness of this method is that its quality is limited by the accuracy of the location supplied by the user. A study on the user location field (Hecht et al., 2011) has previously demonstrated that often users do not provide valid location information, choosing instead to enter pop-culture references in the location field.

Alternatively, research methods have also been proposed to infer the location of a tweet from the content generated by a user. Cheng, Caverlee, and Lee (2010) estimated a Twitter user's city-level location based purely on the content of the user's tweets. Mahmud, Nichols, and Drew (2012) used an ensemble of statistical and heuristic classifiers to infer the home location of Twitter users at different granularity, such as city, state, and time zone, with the content information and Tweeting behavior. Network-based strategies, which harness the information in a user's social connections, may also be used to triangulate their location (Rout et al., 2013). However, these approaches rely on the availability of a user's tweet history, which is not readily available due to the number of users active during a crisis and the constraints imposed by the Twitter API. As an alternative, Kumar, Hu, and Lu (2014b) and Morstatter et al. (2014a) proposed a classification approach to simply decide whether a user was located within the crisis region using various content-based measures and user profile information. This idea generalizes to other scenarios where the exact location of a user does not need to be known and it suffices to know whether the user is in a region of interest or not.

3.2. User Profiling[27]

It has been shown that Twitter opinion could be approached in a manner close to that of traditional polls. However, unlike polls there is little information about individual Twitter users (namely, their demographics and location) and, hence, it is very difficult (not to say impossible) to characterize the group whose opinion one is analyzing. Therefore, to approximate the performance of

---

[21] http://www.geonames.org/.
[22] http://wiki.openstreetmap.org/wiki/Nominatim.
[23] http://developer.mapquest.com/web/products/open/nominatim.
[24] http://msdn.microsoft.com/en-us/library/ff701733.aspx.
[25] https://developers.google.com/maps/documentation/business/geolocation/.
[26] https://developer.yahoo.com/boss/geo/.
[27] Contibuted by Daniel Gayo-Avello.

traditional polls, Twitter data must be enriched to incorporate both the demographic traits and the location of the users whose opinions are being collected.

Demographics are crucial because Twitter user base is not representative of the population as a whole (e.g. Mislove et al., 2011) and, hence, Twitter opinion is the product of a biased sample of that population. Unfortunately, Twitter profiles are extremely terse: the only compulsory field is the user's name (which does not have to be a "real" name); the biographical description, location, and homepage are optional. Notwithstanding, there are users who provide their real names, actual geographical locations and meaningful (albeit brief) biographies. Data from those users provide clues that can be exploited to infer demographic or geographic traits for the rest of users. With regard to the Twitter users' traits that have received more attention from researchers they are: location (at different granularities, i.e. country, state, city, etc.); gender (only male and female), and age (actually age intervals).

Other important traits (given their predictive power, for example, with regard to elections) such as race and ethnicity, religious affiliation, and sexual orientation have been seldom analyzed. Race or ethnicity has been extracted from Twitter data by Gayo Avello (2011); Pennacchiotti and Popescu (2011b); Pennacchiotti and Popescu (2011a); and Bergsma et al. (2013), and just one tried to predict religious affiliation and sexual orientation of Twitter users (Gayo Avello (2011)).

Regarding the precision of user profiling from Twitter data, it greatly depends on the trait of interest. For instance, Gayo Avello (2011) reported a 96% precision for religious affiliation, 100% for sexual orientation, and 70% for race/ethnicity in out-of-sample experiments. In contrast, in-sample experiments (which produced higher precision for the just mentioned traits) obtained 66% precision for gender, and 46% for age.

Nevertheless, precision is not the only performance metric to consider; recall is the other side of the coin. This metric indicates the percentage of relevant items found by a given algorithm. For instance, if we are trying to find lawyers in Twitter, and we obtain a 25% recall it means that there are still 75% of lawyers out there that have not been identified. Following with the same study by Gayo-Avello and out-of-sample experiments, recall for each trait was as follows: religious affiliation 24%, political orientation 33%, sexual orientation 24%, and race/ethnicity 5%. Such low recall values are obviously a problem if one aims to profile every single user on Twitter; however, they are unavoidable to reduce false positives to a minimum.

In brief, inferring demographics for Twitter users with high accuracy is feasible for most of the traits starting with a reasonable amount of labeled data. However, there is a downside: recall is normally low to avoid false positives.

3.3. *Constructing Networks from Twitter Data*

We can employ a network-based approach to answer effectively many of the questions asked of the data. For example, questions such as "who is important?" can be answered by assessing the centrality of a particular user. A discussion of the fundamental components that make up the network can be found in Section 1. More information on centrality measures and approaches to studying social networks can be found in Zafarani, Abbasi, and Liu (2014) and Brandes, Pfeffer, and Mergel (2013).

3.3.1. Retweet Networks

One of the most common interactions between users on Twitter is the retweet action. When one Twitter user retweets another user's tweet, he or she forwards that tweet to all of his or her followers. In this way, the retweet action provides a larger audience to a user's tweet and causes information to flow throughout the Twitter network. While one user can retweet another in a positive or a negative light, there is no doubt that the retweet increases a tweet's (and by extension, a user's) popularity. For this reason, it is useful to study this relationship on Twitter.

The retweet network is asymmetric: one user can retweet another's tweet without that user acknowledging it or retweeting in return. Due to the nature of the retweet, this type of analysis requires a directed graph. While the edges clearly should be directed, the meaning of the nodes is left to the question the analyst wants to answer. It is reasonable in some problems (e.g., information diffusion) to use tweets as nodes and model the graph as a "tweet × tweet" graph. In other problems (e.g., user influence), the appropriate choice may be to model it as a "user × user" graph to understand the users who are retweeted most often. The choice of what a node represents will affect the resulting analysis carried out on the network. An example retweet graph is shown in Figure 1.3. Here, we have chosen users as nodes.

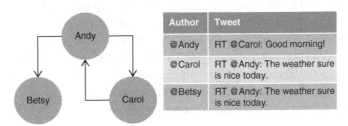

Figure 1.3. A directed retweet graph.
Here, Andy has been retweeted by Betsy and Carol, and Carol has been retweeted by Andy.

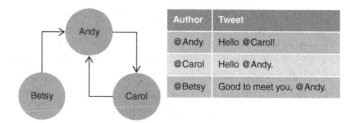

Author	Tweet
@Andy	Hello @Carol!
@Carol	Hello @Andy.
@Betsy	Good to meet you, @Andy.

Figure 1.4. User mentions network.
A directed graph of users mentioning each other in their Tweets.

3.3.2. User Mentions Networks

Another interaction between Twitter users is the user mention (see Figure 1.4). When one user publishes a tweet and wants to mention another user explicitly in his or her tweet, the user includes the other user's Twitter handle in the tweet, prepending it with the @ character. In this way, he or she calls attention to the user being mentioned; the mentioned user will usually be informed of the mention,[28] and this action may initiate a conversation between the users.

The mention network is also asymmetric: one user can mention another user in a tweet without that user acknowledging it or joining in the conversation. This type of interaction also lends itself to a directed graph. Since the user mention is a user interaction (as opposed to a retweet, which is a tweet interaction), it generally makes more sense to build this graph as a "user × user" graph, where each edge represents one user mentioning another. There may be some cases where it is appropriate to model the graph as a "tweet × user" graph, where Tweets are connected to the users that they mention.

3.3.3. Follow Networks

So far, we have described networks that come directly from the text that the users post. These networks can be derived simply by observing what the users write in their tweet. While these networks are important to understanding the underlying dynamics of Twitter, there is another very important part of what goes into communication on Twitter: the social network of friends and followers.

The social network that underpins Twitter is directed: users can follow each other without the need for reciprocity. Because of this, the graph is most typically modeled as a "user × user" network, where directed edges indicate a follow relationship between the two users.

---

[28] For "verified users," typically celebrities, Twitter offers the option to filter mentions to reduce clutter and spam. See https://blog.twitter.com/2013/filtering-mentions.

3.3.4. Content Networks

All of the networks so far rely upon an interaction involving two users: a retweet, a mention, or a follow. In addition to these types of actions, we can also extract networks from the content in a user's tweet to see how the topics in the user's text are connected. One of the most straightforward way to observe the topics a user talks about is to inspect the user's hashtags. Hashtags are special words in a tweet that begin with the # character. What makes hashtags special is that each hashtag has its own special page on Twitter where users can go and contribute to that tag's conversation by including the tag in their tweet. This incentivizes users to include hashtags in their tweet.

One common way to build a content network is to construct a network from the co-occurrence of hashtags in users' tweets. Constructing the network in this way yields an undirected graph with weighted edges, where weights are determined by the number of times the hashtags co-occur in the Twitter corpus. These weights can be used as part of a calculation to determine which hashtags are most important when compared to another hashtag. We present an example of a hashtag network in Figure 1.5.

While hashtags are the most common types of text features that are used to build these networks, any text feature could be substituted to perform similar analysis. For example, we could perform this analysis on named entities, *n*-grams, and so on.

3.3.5. Data Storage and Retrieval

Using the methods for data collection described earlier in this chapter, one can quickly amass a large volume of tweets, tweeters, and network information. It is estimated that as of mid-2014, approximately 500 million tweets are

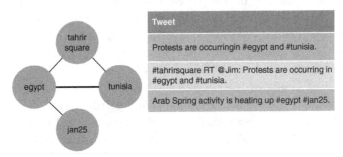

Figure 1.5. A hashtag network.
A hashtag network is constructed by observing which hashtags co-occur in tweets. In the figure, the edge weight is depicted by the thickness of the lines between the nodes. The edge between "egypt" and "tunisia" has a weight of 2, and all other lines have a weight of 1.

generated on Twitter each day, and that number is climbing steadily. With so much data generated on Twitter each day, even a modest query to Twitter's API can yield a plethora of Twitter data.

So far we have assumed that you will store your data in a text-based archive, simply writing the JSON from the APIs to a text file. The drawback to this approach is that managing even a moderate-sized dataset is cumbersome when storing data in a text-based archive, and this solution will not give the performance needed to understand the data in a timely fashion, let alone to support a real-time application. In this chapter, we present some common storage methodologies for Twitter data using a common NoSQL database, MongoDB. There are several NoSQL implementations, including Hadoop.[29] We choose MongoDB[30] as an example NoSQL implementation for its adherence to the following principles:

- **Document-Oriented Storage.** MongoDB organizes its data as a collection of JSON-style objects. This makes it very easy to store raw documents from Twitter's APIs. This also gives the flexibility of not needing to redefine the data schema when Twitter adds or removes fields with different versions of their API.
- **Index Support.** As in many database systems, MongoDB allows for indexes on any field. This makes it easy to create indexes optimized for any application.
- **Straightforward Queries.** True to its nature as a JSON-style document format, MongoDB supports flexible queries in the format of JSON documents. MongoDB's queries, while syntactically much different from SQL, are semantically very similar, making it very easy for a novice to understand. In addition to regular queries, MongoDB supports MapReduce,[31] which makes it easy to aggregate the data.

This chapter does not go through the process of setting up a MongoDB instance. A detailed explanation of this process can be found in Kumar, Morstatter, and Liu (2014a). The following subsections present examples of two simple "tweet count" queries, one using MongoDB's native JavaScript, the another on Apache Hadoop running Pig (Olston et al., 2008). The goal of these queries is to find the users with the most mentions in a Twitter dataset.

3.3.6. Example 1: MongoDB

MongoDB natively supports JSON for each document stored in the database. Furthermore, all commands in MongoDB are written in JavaScript. This makes

---

[29] http://hadoop.apache.org/.
[30] http://www.mongodb.org/.
[31] MapReduce is a programming model for processing large datasets in a distributed setting. A MapReduce program has a Map procedure, typically performing prefiltering and sorting, and is followed by a Reduce procedure, which computes aggregate summaries.

the construction of MapReduce programs straightforward. In Listing 1.2, we see the construction of a MongoDB MapReduce program. mapFunction takes each individual tweet and creates a series of key values of the form "(@user, 1)". These keys and values are then summed in the reducer.

Listing 1.2 *MapReduce program that stores the users and the number of mentions in a separate collection.*

```
> /*
> * This is the map function, which takes a series of
> * tweets and produces a series of key/value pairs.
> * This function extracts each user mentioned,
> * and the count of each mention.
> * The function takes 0 parameters, as the document
> * will be passed through context (the 'this' object).
> */
> var mapFunction = function(){
...       //loop through all of the mentions in the
document.
...        var userMentions = this. entities. user_mentions;
...        for(var i = 0; i < userMentions. length; i ++) {
...          //emit the username (key) and
...          //the count (value , in this case always 1).
...          emit (userMentions [i]. screen_name, 1);
...        }
...    }

> /*
> * This function sums the number of mentions of each user
> */
> var reduceFunction = function(key, mention_counts){
...        return Array.sum(mention_counts);
...}

> //Perform the MapReduce operation, and store the results
> //in a new collection, "users_mentioned_table".
> db. my_tweet_collection . mapReduce (mapFunction ,
       reduceFunction , {"out": "users_mentioned_table"});

> //List the most - mentioned users
> db. users_mentioned_table . find (). sort ({"value": -1})
{"id" : "MostMentionedUser", "value" : 1000}
{"id" : "SecondMostMentioned", "value" : 700}
...
```

3.3.7. Example 2: Pig

Pig sits on top of a Hadoop installation. The language, Pig Latin, abstracts the individual map and reduces commands and instead provides a concise language for building MapReduce applications. An example Pig program is shown in Listing 1.3, which does the same calculation as the MapReduce example.

Listing 1.3 *Pig script that finds the users mentioned and the number of mentions in a separate collection.*

```
grunt > TWEET = LOAD 'my_tweet_collection.json' USING
      JsonLoader ('text : chararray');
grunt > X = FOREACH TWEET GENERATE TOKENIZE (text);
grunt > Y = FOREACH X GENERATE REGEX_
EXTRACT_ALL ('@\w+', $0);
grunt > Z = FOREACH Y GENERATE COUNT ($0);
grunt > DUMP Z;
```

4. Investigating Research Problems Using Twitter Data

Using the various data collected from Twitter, we can investigate myriad research problems. Twitter offers rich data on several types of user behavior, and these behaviors can be observed, analyzed, and predicted using Twitter data. Here we describe some examples of important, basic research underlying many other research tasks.

4.1. *How Do We Assess the Quality of Data Obtained Through the Streaming APIs?*

When collecting data from Twitter directly using its APIs, researchers conduct many studies using the streaming API. Twitter's streaming API returns a sample of tweets from Twitter matching the parameters specified by the user. According to the documentation, the sample will return at most 1 percent of all the tweets produced on Twitter at a given time. Once the number of tweets matching the given parameters eclipses 1 percent of all the tweets on Twitter, Twitter begins to sample the data returned to the user. The method that Twitter employs to sample these data is unpublished. Researchers usually assume that it is an independent, uniform sampling process so that the sample obtained is representative of the complete set of tweets matching the desired criteria. The streaming API takes three parameters: keywords (words, phrases, or hashtags), geographical boundary boxes, and user IDs.

One way to overcome the 1 percent limitation is to use the Twitter Firehose, a feed provided by Twitter that allows access to 100 percent of all public tweets. Access to the Firehose can be obtained in many ways, one of which is by directly buying Firehose access from Twitter. Gnip,[32] a subsidiary of Twitter, is one of these outlets. Another outlet, Datasift,[33] allows users to purchase elevated access to the data. One benefit of these outlets is that they allow a user to obtain historic data, which is currently not supported by Twitter.

A very substantial drawback of these methods is the restrictive cost. Another drawback is the sheer amount of resources required to retain the full 100 percent data (servers, network availability, and disk space). Consequently, those who wish to study these data are forced to decide between two versions of the API: the freely available but limited Streaming, and the very expensive but comprehensive version.

In Morstatter et al. (2013b), the authors assess the streaming API, measuring how representative it is when compared to the Firehose data. They compare the data along two facets commonly studied in many Twitter analyses: the top hashtags, the topics in the corpus, the networks obtained by "user × user" retweet networks (described in Section 3.3.1), and the geographical distribution of geotagged tweets. In their study, they find strong evidence that there is some bias in the top hashtags and the topics in the text. This is important for other studies, as it indicates that the sample might not be representative of all Twitter activity.

4.1.1. Finding Bias in the Streaming API

The first facet that Morstatter et al. (2013b) compare are the top hashtags in the text. The authors compare the correlation in the top hashtags. The results of this analysis are shown in Figure 1.6a. This figure compares the correlation coefficient, $\tau\beta$, at the top hashtag lists of different sizes, called n. Here we see that when n is bigger, the data are well correlated. When n is smaller, however, the correlation varies widely, with some negative correlation on one of the days. This is problematic, as many of the studies carried out on hashtags measure the top hashtags in the data, exactly where we see the issues in the correlation.

One of the questions the authors ask about these results is whether we would normally see this behavior when we sample Twitter data. The authors want to see whether this is a pattern that occurs when sampling the Twitter data or if it is an indication of some underlying bias in the sampling mechanism in the streaming API. To carry out this analysis, the authors compare their streaming API data with one hundred fake streaming API results created by sampling the Firehose data. The authors repeat the analysis on all one hundred samples and obtain the results shown in Figure 1.6b. Here we see nearly perfect positive correlation in the shorter lists, which begin to settle at the longer lists.

---

[32] http://gnip.com/.
[33] http://datasift.com/.

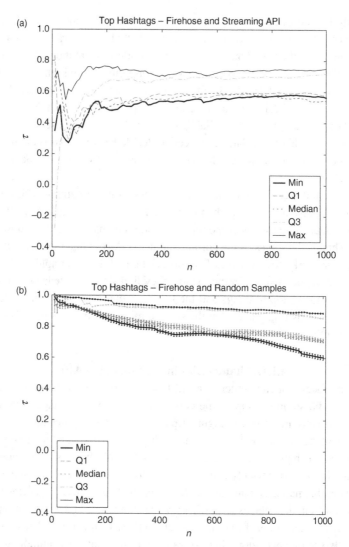

Figure 1.6. A comparison of the correlation of top hashtags in tweets collected using the streaming API and a random sample from Twitter Firehose.
(a) Relationship between n – number of top hashtags, and the correlation coefficient, $\tau\beta$.
(b) Random sampling of Firehose data. Relationship between n – number of top hashtags, and $\tau\beta$ – the correlation coefficient for different levels of coverage.

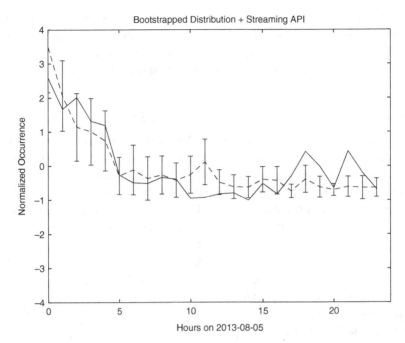

Figure 1.7. Overview of the bootstrapping process that determines time periods of bias in the streaming API.

The solid line represents the trend of a particular hashtag over one day from the streaming API. The dashed line represents the trend of a particular hashtag over one day from the Sample API. Confidence intervals are obtained from the Sample API by bootstrapping. We see periods where the streaming API falls outside of the confidence intervals are biased.

4.1.2. Finding Bias Without the Firehose

Morstatter et al. (2013b) and Morstatter Pfeffer, and Liu (2014b) seek to find time periods of bias by assessing the streaming API response without the need of the Firehose. The authors test the Sample API,[34] another feed provided by Twitter, for its validity as a comparison mechanism. The authors find that the Sample API provides an unbiased sample of Firehose data and use it to find periods of bias in the streaming API.

To compare the two sources, the authors bootstrap the response from the Sample API. By analyzing the data in this way, the authors are able to find time periods of bias and time periods where the data from the streaming API are representative of the data in the Firehose. A brief overview of the process can be seen in Figure 1.7.

---

[34] https://dev.twitter.com/docs/api/1.1/get/statuses/sample.

The results of this work indicate that there is bias in the sampling mechanism from Twitter and that researchers and practitioners should be careful with the data they collect from these outlets. To test whether a collected dataset is biased, one can make use of the method proposed in Morstatter, Pfeffer, and Liu (2014b).

4.2. Sentiment Analysis of Tweets

The goal of sentiment analysis is to determine automatically the opinion expressed in a given document with respect to a target. A typical sentiment analysis/opinion mining system consists of three components (Speriosu et al., 2011): (1) Topic-based information retrieval is used to understand the opinions associated with a topic, such as the Arab Spring. This process involves the collection of data associated with the topic or the target. (2) Subjectivity classification is used to determine whether a given document is objective or subjective. (3) In polarity sentiment classification, the subjective documents identified by the second component are further classified into positive and negative. Although two-class sentiment classification is widely used in sentiment analysis, it is possible to extend it to a multiclass problem, where the polarity is expressed on a gradient.

As an opinion-rich resource, social media has attracted attention from several disciplines to understand the opinions of individuals or gauge aggregated sentiment of mass populations (Amiri & Chua, 2012; Hu et al., 2013a, 2013b). By applying sentiment analysis on the tweets associated with specific events, Bollen, Mao, and Pepe (2011) and Kim et al. (2009) studied events in the social, political, cultural, and economic sphere, and found that the events have a strong effect on public mood.

Distinct characteristics of social media data present new opportunities for sentiment analysis. To accomplish sentiment analysis in social media, Hu et al. (2013a) proposed a sociological approach that used the social network information. The basic idea is to model social relations for sentiment analysis using two social theories: (1) sentiments of two messages posted by the same user are more likely to be more consistent than those of two random messages (sentiment consistency), and (2) sentiments of two messages posted by friends are more likely to be similar than that of two random messages. In addition, abundant emotional signals such as emoticons are observed in social media. Hu et al. (2013b) proposed a unified unsupervised model to capture the emotional signals – that is, emotion indication and emotion correlation – which are strongly correlated with the sentiment expressed in the social media posts. For a more detailed discussion on the state of the art in sentiment analysis on social media data, we refer the readers to Mejova (2012).

Packaged tools are also now available to help with this task. SentiStrength[35] may be used to classify tweets as positively or negatively oriented in fourteen languages. SentiWordNet[36] can be used to identify the opinion of words in the tweet. Using the words from WordNet,[37] a lexical database consisting of related words as concepts, SentiWordNet can classify each word as positive, negative, or objective.

4.3. *Detecting Events in Twitter Data*

Recent crisis events, such as the Westgate Mall attack in Kenya,[38] have shown that Twitter is being increasingly used to publish breaking news. Often this occurs before the news is communicated via traditional news sources. Hence, Twitter is an important source of information to identify discussions surrounding events of significance, such as earthquakes, hurricanes, and other crises. Tweets can be used to coordinate a response or to evaluate the impact of current response efforts. A first step toward this is detecting events and identifying the related discussion on Twitter.

Sakaki, Okazaki, and Matsuo (2010) attempted to detect earthquakes from the information generated by social sensors as represented by the Twitter users. Using both temporal and geospatial models, the authors demonstrated that the tweets could be used to predict earthquakes moments after they occur and even predict an earthquake's location. Similarly, the authors show that it is possible to predict the trajectory of hurricanes using tweets generated from the affected region. In Weng and Lee (2011), the authors leveraged the redundancy in the vocabulary to identify clusters of words that represent events. The authors constructed word signals using the Wavelet Transformation and then used a modularity-based graph-partitioning approach on the correlation matrix containing the correlation between different word signals to obtain clusters of words, which represented events.

This problem can be particularly challenging in Twitter due to the sheer volume of tweets and the dynamicity of the stream. There is also a high volume of noise in the stream, in the form of interpersonal conversations. Thus, an effective event detection solution for Twitter must address these challenges. In Kumar et al. (2014c), the authors present an event detection approach to handle fast, evolving, and noisy Twitter streams. Due to the popularity of smartphones and capable mobile devices, social media users may be considered as sensors.

---

[35] http://sentistrength.wlv.ac.uk/.
[36] http://sentiwordnet.isti.cnr.it/.
[37] http://wordnetweb.princeton.edu/.
[38] http://bigstory.ap.org/article/kenya-attack-unfolded-and-down-twitter-feeds.

Thus, the information generated from each sensor can be aggregated to detect events. Here, the authors propose an incremental clustering method leveraging a compression-based distance measure to aggregate tweets in noisy Twitter streams into events. A temporal model in the approach assists in the capture of evolving events.

5. Tools for Twitter Data Collection and Analysis

Due to the popularity of Twitter and the use of Twitter data in numerous applications, libraries to help in the data collection exist in most popular programming languages. For those interested, an updated list of these libraries can be obtained at the Twitter developer's website.[39] A popular Twitter library for Java is Twitter4J, which provides convenient methods to access the REST APIs. To access the streaming APIs and to scale to the large volume observed in Twitter streams, the Hosebird client is recommended to the readers.

Collecting and analyzing tweets can be challenging. To address this challenge, several applications, both commercial and academic, are being developed to empower users to analyze tweets. NodeXL (Hansen, Shneiderman, & Smith, 2010) is an example of such a tool. This powerful plugin for Microsoft Excel was designed to address the needs of social scientists interested in analyzing social media data. In addition to Twitter, the tool includes a data importer for several social media sources, including Facebook and YouTube, and is able to access directly the data loaded into Excel worksheets. The ingested data can then be visualized in several popular graph layouts. Network measures can be computed on the graph nodes and used to identify influential nodes. The plugin is available as open source software.[40]

Due to the large volume of tweets, manual inspection of tweets is not practical, and automated analysis often is necessary. One of the earliest systems to focus on the information filtering problem in the context of crises is TweetTracker (Kumar et al., 2011), shown in Figure 1.8. The web application facilitates the tracking of emerging events by providing a partially automated mechanism to collect and analyze tweets to obtain situational awareness during a crisis. Events are described as a collection of hashtags and keywords, geographic boundary boxes, and Twitter IDs, and collected tweets are grouped accordingly. Near–real-time analysis of the data is supported via visual analytics, such as the location of the tweets being shown on a map, and the text in the

---

[39] https://dev.twitter.com/docs/twitterlibraries.
[40] http://nodexl.codeplex.com/.

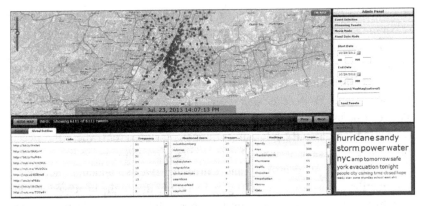

Figure 1.8. A screenshot of the main screen of TweetTracker.
The figure shows the Tweets generated from the New York region during
Hurricane Sandy. Tables below the map summarize the frequently mentioned
users and resources in the Tweets.

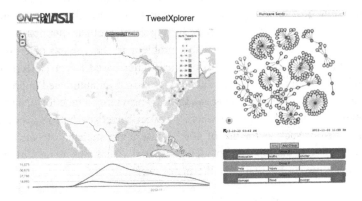

Figure 1.9. A view of the different components of TweetXplorer.
The figure shows information pertaining to three themes.

tweets being summarized using a word cloud. Using the system requires the
registration for an account.[41]

Other systems to analyze tweets visually include TweetXplorer (Morstatter
et al., 2013a), which may be used to visualize and analyze events using Twitter.
TweetXplorer (see Figure 1.9) supports analysis of Twitter data from the following perspectives: temporal, geospatial, network, and text. Analysis of the
tweets is organized along user-defined themes. Visual analytics include the

---

[41] Tweet Tracker Registration URL: http://bit.ly/TT-reg.

information propagation network to identify important users and a heatmap to summarize important geographic regions pertaining to the themes. The Twitris[42] system may also be used to monitor events such as natural disasters. Visual analytics indicate relevant regions containing popular terms related to an event. Tweets from an event can also be recorded to investigate later along with relevant articles from other sources such as news and Wikipedia. Sentiment viz[43] can be used to visualize the sentiment around a keyword. Additionally, the system can identify relevant geographic regions from where the tweets originate and observe groups of tweets centered on common topics.

The problem of identifying and extracting Tweets containing actionable information is particularly challenging in Twitter due to the increased volume of available information. An innovative approach to address this problem was proposed in Starbird and Stamberger (2010). The Tweak the Tweet project designed a paradigm to efficiently annotate vital information such as the location of an incident or the type of an incident during a crisis to facilitate the extraction of actionable information.[44]

Events are usually unexpected, and it has been observed that Twitter can be the source of breaking news, sometimes before traditional news sources. Therefore, detecting such events is an important problem for first responders. Li et al. (2012) investigated this problem in the context of crime and disaster-related events (CDEs) using the Twitter-based Event Detection and Analysis System (TEDAS). The authors proposed an automated approach to classify new tweets as belonging to a CDE by providing a function to classify a tweet from by its nature, such as whether a tweet is a retweet and disaster-related characteristics such as the use of numbers to report statistics. To analyze the detected tweets, the system provided geospatial visual aids along with querying capabilities to facilitate the filtering of tweets.

Acknowledgments

This work was supported, in part, by the Office of Naval Research grant N000141410095 and Minerva grant N000141310835. The authors would also like to thank Xia (Ben) Hu for his contribution to the discussion on sentiment analysis using Twitter data.

---

[42] http://twitris.knoesis.org/yolandastorm2013/.
[43] http://www.csc.ncsu.edu/faculty/healey/tweet_viz/tweet_app/.
[44] An example of such annotated information can be observed from the tweets generated during Hurricane Irene in 2012 at http://www.cs.colorado.edu/~starbird/TtT_Irene_map_byEvent.html.

References

Amiri, Hadi, and Chua, Tat-Seng. 2012. Mining slang and urban opinion words and phrases from cQA services: an optimization approach. In *Proceedings of the Fifth ACM International Conference on Web Search and Data Mining. WSDM '12* (pp. 193–202). ACM.

Bergsma, Shane, Dredze, Mark, Van Durme, Benjamin, Wilson, Theresa, and Yarowsky, David. 2013. Broadly Improving User Classification via Communication-Based Name and Location Clustering on Twitter (pp.1010–1019). HLT-NAACL.

Bollen, Johan, Mao, Huina, and Pepe, Alberto. 2011. Modeling public mood and emotion: Twitter sentiment and socio-economic phenomena. In *Proceedings of the Fifth International AAAI Conference on Weblogs and Social Media. ICWSM '11* (pp. 450–3). AAAI.

Bontcheva, Kalina, Derczynski, Leon, Funk, Adam, Greenwood, Mark A., Maynard, Diana, and Aswani, Niraj. 2013. TwitIE: an open-source information extraction pipeline for microblog text. In *Proceedings of the International Conference on Recent Advances in Natural Language Processing* (pp. 83–90). Association for Computational Linguistics.

Brandes, Ulrik, Pfeffer, Jürgen, and Mergel, Ines. 2013. *Studying Social Networks: A Guide to Empirical Research.* Campus Verlag.

Cheng, Zhiyuan, Caverlee, James, and Lee, Kyumin. 2010. You are where you tweet: a content-based approach to geo-locating Twitter users. In *Proceedings of the Nineteenth ACM International Conference on Information and Knowledge Management. CIKM '10* (pp. 759–68). ACM.

Gayo-Avello, D. (2011). All liaisons are dangerous when all your friends are known to us. In *Proceedings of the 22nd ACM Conference on Hypertext and Hypermedia* (pp. 171–180). ACM.

Hansen, Derek, Shneiderman, Ben, and Smith, Marc. 2010. *Analyzing Social Media Networks with NodeXL: Insights from a Connected World.* Morgan Kaufmann.

Hecht, Brent, Hong, Lichan, Suh, Bongwon, and Chi, Ed. 2011. Tweets from Justin Bieber's heart: the dynamics of the location field in user profiles. In *Proceedings of the SIGCHI Conference on Human Factors in Computing Systems* (pp. 237–46). ACM.

Hu, Xia, Tang, Jiliang, Gao, Huiji, and Liu, Huan. 2013b. Unsupervised sentiment analysis with emotional signals. In *Proceedings of the 22nd International Conference on World Wide Web. WWW'13.* (pp. 607–18). International World Wide Web Conferences Steering Committee.

Hu, Xia, Tang, Lei, Tang, Jiliang, and Liu, Huan. 2013a. Exploiting social relations for sentiment analysis in microblogging. In *Proceedings of the Sixth ACM International Conference on Web Search and Data Mining* (pp. 537–46). ACM.

Kim, Elsa, Gilbert, Sam, Edwards, Michael J, and Graeff, Erhardt. 2009. Detecting sadness in 140 characters: sentiment analysis and mourning Michael Jackson on Twitter. *Web Ecology*, 3, 1–15.

Kumar, Shamanth, Barbier, Geoffrey, Abbasi, Mohammad Ali, and Liu, Huan. 2011. TweetTracker: an analysis tool for humanitarian and disaster relief. In *Proceedings of 5th AAAI International Conference on Weblogs and Social Media* (pp. 661–2). AAAI.

Kumar, Shamanth, Morstatter, Fred, and Liu, Huan. 2014a. *Twitter Data Analytics*. SpringerBriefs in Computer Science.

Kumar, Shamanth, Hu, Xia, and Liu, Huan. 2014b. A behavior analytics approach to identifying tweets from crisis regions. In *Proceedings of the 25th ACM Conference on Hypertext and Social Media. HT '14* (pp. 555–6). ACM.

Kumar, Shamanth, Liu, Huan, Mehta, Sameep, and Subramaniam, L Venkata. 2014c. From tweets to events: exploring a scalable solution for Twitter streams. arXiv preprint arXiv:1405.1392.

Li, Rui, Lei, Kin Hou, Khadiwala, Ravi, and Chang, Kevin Chen-Chuan. 2012. TEDAS: A Twitter-based Event Detection and Analysis System. In *2012 IEEE 28th International Conference on Data Engineering (ICDE)* (pp. 1273–6). IEEE.

Mahmud, Jalal, Nichols, Jeffrey, and Drews, Clemens. 2012. Where is this tweet from? Inferring home locations of Twitter users. In *Proceedings of the Sixth International AAAI Conference on Weblogs and Social Media. ICWSM '12* (pp. 511–14). AAAI.

Mejova, Yelena Aleksandrovna. 2012. *Sentiment Analysis Within and Across Social Media Streams*. Ph.D. thesis, University of Iowa.

Mislove, A., Lehmann, S., Ahn, Y. Y., Onnela, J. P., & Rosenquist, J. N. (2011). Understanding the demographics of Twitter users. *ICWSM*, 11 (5).

Morstatter, F., Kumar, S., Liu, H., and Maciejewski, R. 2013a. Understanding Twitter data with TweetXplorer. In *Proceedings of the 19th ACM SIGKDD International Conference on Knowledge Discovery and Data Mining* (pp. 1482–5). ACM.

Morstatter, Fred, Pfeffer, Jürgen, Liu, Huan, and Carley, Kathleen. 2013b. Is the sample good enough? Comparing data from Twitter's streaming API with Twitter's Firehose. In *Proceedings of the International Conference on Weblogs and Social Media* (pp. 23–7). Association for Computational Linguistics.

Morstatter, Fred, Lubold, Nichola, Pon-Barry, Heather, Pfeffer, Jürgen, and Liu, Huan. 2014a. Finding eyewitness tweets during crises. In *Proceedings of the ACL 2014 Workshop on Language Technologies and Computational Social Science* (pp. 23–7). Association for Computational Linguistics.

Morstatter, Fred, Pfeffer, Jürgen, and Liu, Huan. 2014b. When is it biased? Assessing the representativeness of Twitter's streaming API. In *Proceedings of the Companion Publication of the 23rd International Conference on World Wide Web Companion. WWW Companion '14* (pp. 555–6). International World Wide Web Conferences Steering Committee.

Olston, Christopher, Reed, Benjamin, Srivastava, Utkarsh, Kumar, Ravi, and Tomkins, Andrew. 2008. Pig Latin: A not-so-foreign language for data processing. In *Proceedings of the 2008 ACM SIGMOD International Conference on Management of Data. SIGMOD '08* (pp. 1099–1110). ACM.

Owoputi, Olutobi, O'Connor, Brendan, Dyer, Chris, Gimpel, Kevin, Schneider, Nathan, and Smith, Noah. 2013. Improved part-of-speech tagging for online conversational text with word clusters. In *Proceedings of NAACL-HLT* (pp. 380–90). Association for Computational Linguistics.

Pennacchiotti, M., & Popescu, A. M. (2001a). Democrats, Republicans and Starbucks afficionados: user classification in Twitter. In *Proceedings of the 17th ACM SIGKDD International Conference on Knowledge Discovery and Data Mining* (pp. 430–8). ACM.

Pennacchiotti, M. & Popescu, A. M. (2001b). A machine learning approach to Twitter user classification. In *Proceedings of the Fifth International AAAI Conferences on Weblogs and Social Media* (pp. 281–8). AAAI Press.

Ritter, Alan, Clark, Sam, Mausam, and Etzioni, Oren. 2011. Named entity recognition in tweets: an experimental study. In *Proceedings of the Conference on Empirical Methods in Natural Language Processing. EMNLP '11* (pp. 1524–34). Association for Computational Linguistics.

Rout, Dominic, Bontcheva, Kalina, Preotiuc-Pietro, Daniel, and Cohn, Trevor. 2013. Where's @Wally? A classification approach to geolocating users based on their social ties. In *24th ACM Conference on Hypertext and Social Media* (pp. 11–20). ACM.

Sakaki, Takeshi, Okazaki, Makoto, and Matsuo, Yutaka. 2010. Earthquake shakes Twitter users: real-time event detection by social sensors. In *Proceedings of the 19th International Conference on World Wide Web* (pp. 851–60). International World Wide Web Conferences Steering Committee.

Speriosu, Michael, Sudan, Nikita, Upadhyay, Sid, and Baldridge, Jason. 2011. Twitter polarity classification with label propagation over lexical links and the follower graph. In *Proceedings of the First Workshop on Unsupervised Learning in NLP* (pp. 53–63). Association for Computational Linguistics.

Starbird, Kate, and Stamberger, Jeannie. 2010. Tweak the tweet: leveraging micro-blogging proliferation with a prescriptive syntax to support citizen reporting. In *Proceedings of Information Systems for Crisis Response and Management (ISCRAM)* (pp. 1071–80). ACM.

Tumasjan, Andranik, Sprenger, Timm Oliver, Sandner, Philipp, and Welpe, Isabell. 2010. Predicting elections with Twitter: what 140 characters reveal about political sentiment. *ICWSM*, 10, 178–85.

Weng, Jianshu, and Lee, Bu-Sung. 2011. Event detection in Twitter. In *Proceedings of the Fifth International AAAI Conference on Weblogs and Social Media. ICWSM '11* (pp. 401–8). AAAI.

Zafarani, Reza, Abbasi, Mohammad Ali, and Liu, Huan. 2014. *Social Media Mining: An Introduction*. Cambridge University Press.

2

Political Opinion

Daniel Gayo-Avello

Despite being a fairly recent phenomenon, microblogging has attracted a large number of researchers and practitioners who consider microposts a suitable source of data to ascertain public opinion. Among the reasons for that interest, we may find the fact that one single platform (i.e., Twitter) is the default choice for users; the ease with which one can collect data using public application programming interfaces (APIs); and the brevity of microposts, which forces users to get to the point when discussing any given topic.

This chapter is focused on efforts to exploit Twitter data to scrutinize public opinion in general, and political discussion in particular. It covers representative case studies conducted during the late 2000s and early 2010s and discusses their respective limitations. Finally, we analyze the implications of such approaches to political opinion in Twitter and depict important lines of research to further advance the field.

1. Introduction

This chapter is devoted to the problem of exploiting Twitter data to take the pulse of public opinion, particularly with regard to electoral forecasting. However, most of the arguments exposed here are not limited to Twitter, but apply broadly to any social networking site.

Twitter is (at the moment of this writing) the most convenient way to obtain user-generated content of opinionated nature about current events. That is the main reason why so much research has been performed on that platform and, in turn, such high expectations have been put on mining Twitter data.

For an in-depth overview of Twitter, in particular its historical evolution, consult the work by Van Dijck (2013, pp. 68–88). Rogers (2013) also analyzes Twitter's evolution, but mainly from a research perspective. His work shows the way in which research has evolved together with the service. In this regard, he provides compelling arguments to drop, once and for all, the caricatured image of Twitter as "pointless babble" and to acknowledge finally that it "serves as a mean to study cultural conditions." Indeed, that simple idea pervades this chapter and the rest of the book.

Not only in the case of Twitter but with regard to public opinion in general, there is no general agreement on its nature, much less on a definition. Broadly stated, there are two opposing perspectives: one held by professional pollsters and another provided by social and political scientists. One of the best comparisons of both points of view was provided by Miller (1995, p. 107), who described both communities as "insiders" and "outsiders," respectively:

> [T]he public for industry outsiders means an interacting group, focused on matters of common interest. [...] The opinions expressed by this sort of public are characterized as reasoned, informed, and genuine. [...] [For insiders] the public is a population of individuals who may have an opinion [...] [T]he public in a given survey is a sample of this larger population of eligible individuals. Some of the opinions in these opinion aggregates may be informed, intense, and policy directed, while others may be ignorant or ephemeral.

We proceed by describing each perspective with some more detail. In this way, we try to ascertain which kind of public opinion Twitter holds and, in turn, which kind of analysis can be conducted on such data.

The "outsiders" perspective is mainly based on the concept of the public sphere (Habermas, 1991): the realm where individuals meet to debate matters concerning all of them to reach a consensus, that is, to shape public opinion. In this regard, public opinion is relevant because it influences the political class – not necessarily driving its decisions, but many times opposing them.

Such idealized description actually corresponds to what Habermas described as the bourgeois public sphere and which, quite obviously, did not include all of the population at that time. In fact, Habermas argued that such a model does not fit well with industrialized societies and, thus, the principles underlying the public sphere were weakened during the twentieth century. First of all, debate was no longer taking place between individuals but mediated through different means (mainly the mass media). Furthermore, the expansion of the public sphere beyond the bourgeoisie implied that the public was less cohesive and, thus, different groups of interest arose, each one trying to drive public opinion to leverage its influence on the political class.

With regard to the "insiders" perspective, the requirements for opinion originally established by Allport (1937) provide a good insight: Opinions are verbalizations produced by many individuals with regard to some object or situation that is important to them; those individuals are usually aware that others are reacting to the same object, but they do not need to be physically close; and, finally, the behaviors are strong enough to have some chance to attain their objectives.

No matter the perspective, public opinion exerts some influence on public matters and, because of that, its analysis is relevant. Furthermore, Allport's requirements for opinion can be rather straightforwardly applied to opinionated tweets. So, from a polling perspective, there is no doubt that Twitter can provide insights regarding public opinion –at least in theory. Whether that opinion qualifies as Habermas' public opinion is another matter. Still, a thorough discussion about the relation between the Twittersphere and the Habermasian public sphere is beyond the scope of this chapter.

In this regard, the interested reader is recommended to consult the works by Dean (2003, 2013) and Freelon (2010, 2013). The former coined the concept of "communicative capitalism," which, according to her definition, is an economic-ideological form that exploits communication to "enrich the few as it placates and diverts the many." Indeed, Dean claims that online services (such as Twitter) are "by design" incapable to fulfill democratic ideals or to boost political debate.

Freelon, in contrast, argues that trying to determine whether the Internet provides a single deliberative space or a set of isolated spheres is pointless. Thus, he proposes a framework comprising of three different approaches to democratic discourse: the liberal individualist, the communitarian, and the deliberative. According to Freelon (2013), Twitter seems to be especially well suited for communitarian discourse, and hence Twitter opinion would not properly fit public opinion from a Habermasian perspective.

2. Mining the Twittersphere for Public Opinion

Twitter opinion may not be Habermas' public opinion, but it somewhat qualifies for the requirements of public opinion polling. From that point of view, this type of opinion can be rather straightforwardly obtained and interpreted, and, in fact, virtually all of the research conducted on Twitter opinion follows (either explicitly or implicitly) a polling approach. Such a perspective is the one covered in this chapter.

In this regard, a significant part of Twitter opinion is consumer opinion (e.g., Jansen et al., 2009; Asur & Huberman, 2010; or Wong, Sen, & Chiang, 2012); however, this chapter is not interested in such a variety, but in opinion about political issues. This section briefly covers a number of representative research works in that line, paying special attention to the particular subtopic of Twitter-based electoral forecasting.

For instance, Diakopoulos and Shamma (2010) analyzed the response of Twitter audiences to televised presidential debates. Their approach was not aimed at determining whether the topics discussed by the candidates resonated with their audience, but instead to find the sentiment response (positive or negative) to each candidate and his or her respective "performance."

Bollen, Mao, and Pepe (2010, 2011) described a method to automatically determine the different mood states of the population (e.g., tension, depression, or anger) and their correlation with different events with presumed societal impact (such as elections, holidays, or disasters). A similar method was later developed by Lansdall-Welfare, Lampos, and Cristianini (2012).

Similarly, O'Connor et al. (2010) studied the correlation between sentiment in tweets and different surveys regarding consumer confidence and presidential job approval, finding that Twitter data positively correlated with such indices (see Figure 2.1). Later work by Marchetti-Bowick and Chambers (2012) also focused on the correlation between sentiment in tweets and presidential job approval.

Finally, some work also exists on different automatic and semiautomatic approaches to detect burst of social tension from Twitter data (e.g., Burnap et al., forthcoming). This chapter does not cover such work, which is only partially related to public opinion mining.

The subfield of Twitter-based opinion analysis that has attracted the most research is, with little doubt, that of electoral forecasting. Certainly, Twitter-based forecasting has been explored in other domains (cf. Schoen et al., 2013; or Kalampokis, Tambouris, & Tarabanis, 2013) but the feasibility of Twitter data to forecast electoral results is still controversial. It is not this author's aim to provide an extensive survey on the topic – to that end, see Gayo-Avello (2013); instead, representative works will be covered to provide a broad picture of the state of the art during the early 2010s.

The first published work describing an attempt to forecast electoral results from Twitter data was made by Tumasjan et al. (2010). These researchers claimed that such kind of a prediction was not only possible but quite straightforward. Their method involved the following steps: (1) choose an election, (2) select keywords corresponding to parties and candidates running for

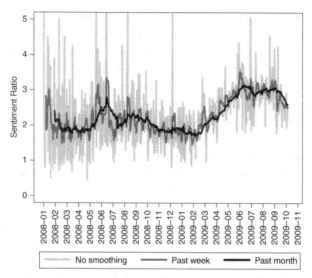

Figure 2.1. Moving averages for the sentiment ratio for the keyword "jobs" under different windows.
From Tweets to Polls: Linking Text Sentiment to Public Opinion Time Series. O'Connor, B., Balasubramanyan, R., Routledge, B. R., and Smith, N. A. In *Proceedings of the International Conference on Weblogs and Social Media*, Figure 5, page 125, © 2010. Association for the Advancement of Artificial Intelligence.

election (but with prior presence in the elected body), (3) collect tweets during a period of time preceding the election, (4) count the number of tweets mentioning each party or candidate, and (5) use the share of tweets for each party or candidate to forecast the share of votes. Tumasjan et al. applied that method to the German elections held in 2009 and claimed it attained quite a competitive performance when compared with traditional polls.

That method has a number of intriguing aspects. First, it does not involve opinion analysis at all; that is, it seems that the polarity of the mentions (i.e., whether they are positive or negative toward the party or candidate) is irrelevant.[1] Second, there are a number of decisions that must be made beforehand, such as the parties to be considered, the keywords to use to track those parties and candidates, and the concrete period of data collection. Yet Tumasjan et al. provided little guidance with regard to the criteria practitioners should apply toward making those decisions.

Indeed, Jungherr, Jürgens, and Schoen (2012) applied the same method to comparable data from the same elections with very different results. For instance, if all of the parties running for election were considered, the

---

[1]   A recent work covered later in this chapter has made similar claims: DiGrazia et al. (2013).

Pirate Party would have been the predicted winner.[2] Similarly, the method's performance was highly dependent on the chosen period of data collection, and because of this Jungherr, Jürgens, and Schoen strongly criticized the work by Tumasjan et al.

After the work by Tumasjan et al., a number of papers covering attempts to forecast elections by using more or less elaborated methods have been produced (e.g., Bermingham & Smeaton, 2011; Livne et al., 2011; Borondo et al., 2012; Sang & Bos, 2012; Skoric et al., 2012; Ceron et al., 2013; or Caldarelli et al., 2014). Most of them have not relied on tweet counts, but instead have performed sentiment analysis to some degree and have trained on manually labeled data. Results have been mixed: none of those works were able to outperform traditional polls, and moreover, although they tend to attain rather accurate results for major parties, forecasts for small parties are prone to large errors. Additional details about the limitations of these approaches are provided in a later subsection.

A common feature of virtually all of those methods is that they solely rely on Twitter data; that is, they do not resort to any additional source of information to make the forecasts. Such an approach is not the most usual one used in other domains; instead, it is common to build models to transform time series produced from online data into time series obtained from other sources. Such models are fit using as input both online data (such as web searches or tweets) and contemporary data collected in traditional ways. Once the model is obtained and no more contemporary data are available, online data are fed into the model to produce the forecasts.

Such an approach has been used to forecast (actually, nowcast) a number of phenomena (e.g., unemployment claims or influenza incidence) from diverse inputs such as web searches or tweets (e.g., Ginsberg et al., 2009; Lampos, De Bie, & Cristianini, 2010; Signorini, Segre, & Polgreen, 2011; Choi & Varian, 2012). Needless to say, in order to be applied to the domain of electoral forecasting, time-evolving data from pre-electoral polls are required. In fact, such an approach to Twitter-based electoral forecasting was already initiated in the early 2010s. Representative work in this line of research was conducted by Shi et al. (2012); Lampos (2012); Lampos, Preotiuc-Pietro, and Cohn (2013); Huberty (2013b); and Beauchamp (2014) (see Figure 2.2). Each of these efforts show promising results.

---

[2] Jungherr, Jürgens, and Schoen (2012) collected tweets containing either a German party or politically loaded words. Those referring to the Pirate Party amounted for 34.8 percent of the whole dataset, thus making the Pirate Party (largely known for fighting Internet regulation) the most tweeted party and, hence, the "winner" of the election. This party was not included in the analysis of Tumasjan et al. (2010), who considered only those parties already represented in the German parliament.

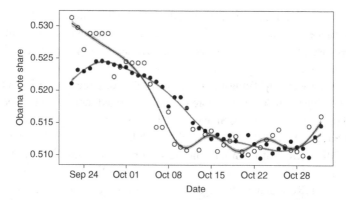

Figure 2.2. Predicted and actual polling for Ohio during the 2012 U.S. presidential elections. Open circles are polls, and filled circles are Twitter-based predictions. (Beauchamp, 2014).

3. Limitations of Previous Methods to Mine Twitter Political Opinion

3.1. *Limitations Due to Approaching Twitter Data from a Pollster's Perspective*

As it has been discussed, most attempts to analyze political opinion in Twitter consider the problem akin to an online survey. Such an approach has two main issues. On one hand, any criticism against public opinion polling can be straightforwardly applied to Twitter-based methods. On the other hand, assumptions that hold for surveys may not entirely apply to Twitter, particularly given its adversarial nature.

Regarding the first issue, there exists abundant literature criticizing opinion polling, but the fierce argumentation by Bourdieu (1979, p. 125) captures the most common arguments:

- Some assumptions are misguided – for instance, that everyone can have an opinion, that all opinions have the same value, and that there is a consensus in society about the problems that deserve attention.
- "No replies" provide invaluable information about the political or conflicting nature of the questions asked in the poll, even more than actual replies.
- The most important function of opinion polls is not to ascertain public opinion, but, in fact, "to impose the illusion that a public opinion exists, and that it is simply the sum of a number of individual opinions."

Such criticisms can be somewhat translated to Twitter and social media:

- Virtually all approaches to determine Twitter opinion have previously defined the topics of interest (by means of keywords or hashtags) instead of discovering them from the available data.

- Because of the automated nature of opinion mining methods, all tweets are treated as equivalent (e.g., issues such as their factuality or their provenance are simply ignored, or tweets from users who rarely make political statements are given the same weight as tweets from politically active users).
- The opinion of those not tweeting about a given topic is, obviously, unknown, and vocal minorities seem to dominate Twitter opinion (see, for instance, Mustafaraj et al., 2011).
- Twitter-derived public opinion can be seen as opportunity to tamper with opinion of the general public, and not only with that of Twitter users. As Metaxas and Mustafaraj (2012, p. 473) put it: "we should expect that all candidates and political parties will use social media sites to [...] influence our perception of candidates (or our perception of their popularity)."

Indeed, one of the major problems of the "pollster approach" to Twitter is due to its adversarial nature. It is true that opinionated tweets can look strikingly similar to opinions in surveys, but they are not, for a very simple reason: while opinions are produced by individuals (Allport, 1937), tweets can be machine-generated. Actually, automated accounts are a notable challenge for anyone trying to mine opinions from Twitter under the assumption that all tweets are human-made (Tufekci, 2014). Given its negative impact, there is a growing body of literature on this topic (e.g., Chu et al., 2010; Zhang & Paxson, 2011; or Tavares & Faisal, 2013).

3.2. *Limitations Due to the Different Sources of Bias in Twitter*

In addition to criticism because of the "pollster approach," some researchers have expressed further concerns regarding the issues of big data approaches. For instance, Huberty (2015, p. 5) quite graphically depicts most methods to perform Twitter-based opinion mining as "purely digital exhaust approaches." In other words, those methods ingest raw tweets without any filtering to produce an output (such as a forecast) with little processing. Huberty argues that, to work properly and consistently, such techniques require implausible assumptions about the nature of the "digital exhaust data." Such assumptions include that virtually everyone has an online presence, that their online presence is consistent with their offline behavior, and that it is persistent for long periods of time. Or, as others have put it, the assumption is that N = all, something that is simply not true (see also Mislove et al., 2011).

   This representativeness issue is mainly due to demographic bias in the Twitter user base. Still, there are additional sources of bias when collecting Twitter data. For instance, Tufekci (2014) has expressed concern regarding the sensitivity of any analysis to the keywords chosen to collect the data. That is, different keywords produce different datasets and potentially different views of the same issue. Given that the keywords chosen to compile that kind of dataset are chosen by researchers, this could be considered a particular case of experimenter's bias (or even data dredging).

Despite the impact of both sources of bias, one of the most important limitations of Twitter data is due to the self-selection bias, which is highly related to the "no replies" criticism by Bourdieu. Twitter users decide which topics they tweet about, the hashtags they use, and the tweets they retweet. Those actions produce data that are observable; however, when users decide not to tweet about a topic, or not to use a given hashtag when discussing a particular issue, or not to retweet something although they have seen it, such actions are invisible to the researchers but still meaningful. Self-selection bias has been insistently exposed and caution is advised (e.g., Gayo-Avello, 2011b, 2012, 2013; Mustafaraj et al., 2011; Mitchell & Hitlin, 2013; Schoen et al., 2013; or Tufekci, 2014).

The preceding issues affect Twitter as a whole; however, most researchers do not have access to the whole user graph or the full Firehose (the data stream containing every published tweet). Most researchers rely on the data provided by the free (gratis) APIs or, at most, the so-called Decahose stream, which provides, for a fee, 10 percent of the published tweets. The possible bias in those sources of data has not been analyzed until quite recently, and the conclusions are problematic: Morstatter et al. (2013) have shown that the streaming API employed by the great majority of researchers does not provide a representative sample of Twitter as a whole.

A number of the aforementioned issues can be avoided, at least partially. For instance, representativeness problems and demographic biases can be reduced by performing user profiling and geolocation. Such tasks are challenging, but they are certainly attainable. Except for a few exceptions, prior works have neglected demographic bias in Twitter data, and this author would like to emphasize the imperative need to produce accurate user profiles, particularly when mining political opinion. After all, voter turnout and political leaning are related to demographic traits such as gender,[3] age,[4] race and ethnicity,[5] religion,[6]

---

[3] Wolfinger (1980); Shapiro & Mahajan (1986); Conover (1988); Leighley & Nagler (1992); Seltzer, Newman, & Leighton (1997); or Green, Palmquist, & Schickler (2004).

[4] Wolfinger (1980); or Wattenberg (2008).

[5] Leighley & Nagler (1992); Tate (1994); Tam (1995); DeSipio (1998); or Green, Palmquist, & Schickler (2004).

[6] Green, Palmquist, & Schickler (2004); Green et al., (2005); Olson & Green (2006); Campbell & Monson (2008); Barreto & Bozonelos (2009); or Jalalzai (2009).

and sexual orientation,[7] and also to geographical traits[8] such as living in urban, suburban, or rural settings. The reader is encouraged to consult Chapter 1 for a thorough discussion of the different approaches to determine both demographic traits and the location of Twitter users.

3.3. *Limitations Due to Common Approaches to Automated Content Analysis*

Automated tools are the only way to perform content analysis on millions of tweets. In fact, the application of such tools in political science is not new, and it can be traced to the foundational work by Laver, Benoit, and Garry (2003), who devised the Wordscore method, a technique that involves the following steps: (1) select a corpus of reference texts with a priori known positions (e.g., within the left–right continuum); (2) compute scores for words appearing in the corpus; (3) score texts with unknown positions using the word scores; (4) and transform text scores into positions within the original spectrum.

Certainly, state-of-the-art methods are much more complex – the reader is recommended to consult Chapter 1 – yet the underlying assumptions and processing stages are still comparable. Using such approaches, the work described in the previous section is able to capture the overall mood or sentiment level of Twitter users with regard to some issue; however, such methods are not able to obtain strongly structured opinions. This should not be a problem provided there are additional sources of data against which a Twitter-based model could be fit.

The more worrisome limitation is due to the way in which opinion mining has been approached in most of the foundational works devoted to political analysis of tweets. Firstly, a number of them claimed that sentiment analysis is not even needed, and that mere tweet counts are enough (e.g., Tumasjan et al., 2010). Secondly, plenty of works relied on simple approaches to sentiment analysis, such as employing general-purpose sentiment lexicons, which, as we discuss later, have serious limitations.

Regarding the feasibility of completely ignoring opinion in political tweets, on one hand, just half of the reports relying on tweet counts were able to forecast electoral results correctly (cf. Gayo-Avello, 2013). Besides, since such forecasts were made *post facto*, we cannot know if such overall results were due to mere chance (as argued by Metaxas, Mustafaraj, & Gayo-Avello, 2011) or unintended data dredging.

---

[7] Sherrill (1996); Hertzog (1996, pp. 51–95); or Bailey (2013, pp. 97–136).
[8] Glenn & Hill (1977); Sauerzopf & Swanstrom (1999); Gainsborough (2001, pp. 66–79); or Walks (2006).

On another hand, a couple of studies have shown that a correlation certainly exists between tweet counts and electoral outcomes. DiGrazia et al. (2013) found a significant positive correlation between tweets mentioning a candidate and the margin of difference between that candidate and his or her opponent, even after controlling for all confounding variables. However, the correlation is subtle, especially when compared with other predictive features, such as incumbency. Similar results were achieved by Jensen and Anstead (2013), who provided a cautious and highly visual illustration of Twitter's predictive power with regard to elections:

> Twitter may be a valuable tool for identifying change and continuity in the state of an electoral campaign. However, the proper metaphor may be less analogous to traditional polling and more like a canary in a coal mine.

Hence, given that tweet volume is only subtly correlated with actual vote margins, and only half of the reports relying on tweet volume were able to make correct forecasts, it is not recommended to rely on mere tweet counts as a proxy for political opinion; some method of sentiment analysis is required. One of the simplest and most popular approaches is based on lexicons. Simply put, they are lists of words with associated scores that are applied to the unknown texts and, that way, their polarity is determined.

Producing such lexicons and determining the corresponding scores are not easy tasks, and most researchers rely on a reduced number of lexicons that can be considered de facto standards. Examples include ANEW (Bradley & Lang, 1999); the one prepared by Wilson, Wiebe, and Hoffmann (2005); and Sentiwordnet (Esuli & Sebastiani, 2006).

The biggest problem of lexicons is that the polarity of words is context-dependent (Turney, 2002), and when users apply lexicons that are not targeted at a given domain (in this case, political opinion), results are unsatisfactory. For instance, Metaxas, Mustafaraj, and Gayo-Avello (2011) showed that the lexicon by Wilson, Wiebe, and Hoffmann (2005), which has been commonly used since its application by O'Connor et al. (2010), is not a feasible choice for political texts. First, it is just slightly better than a random classifier; second, it is unable to deal with misleading information and propaganda; and, finally, sentiment predicted on its basis fails to predict political orientation of Twitter users.

Hence, much better approaches to sentiment analysis are required, and in this regard, the reader is referred to Chapter 1 and the work by Mejova (2012). But even when using state-of-the-art sentiment analysis methods, a note of caution must be sounded because of the idiosyncrasies of political opinion.

On one hand, political opinion is plagued with irony and double entendres that can be difficult to handle with sentiment analysis methods. Thus, while negative material is usually detected with high precision, positive statements often contain a substantial amount of ironic comments that should not be considered positive at all. Indeed, according to Carvalho et al. (2009), up to 35 percent of presumed positive opinions are of an ironic nature. Their work and that by Reyes, Rosso, and Buscaldi (2012) provide a starting point for anyone interested in ironic content detection.

On the other hand, a substantial amount of political opinion expresses an apparently neutral sentiment, and this part of political discourse consists of concrete chosen words that provide clues regarding the user's actual opinion (Yu, Kaufmann, & Diermeier, 2008). In fact, Yu et al. argue that sentiment analysis is not enough to determine political opinion, and that prior knowledge about the user's political orientation is pertinent.

So automated political opinion mining is a much harder problem than general opinion mining. Indeed, at the moment of this writing, it has been shown that the highest accuracy that can be achieved when determining opinion in political tweets is about 60 percent, even after omitting sarcastic material (Bakliwal et al., 2013). Consequently, it is unavoidable not only to improve the accuracy of opinion mining targeted at political texts, but also to infer the political orientation of the authors of those texts.

In this regard, researchers have made several of attempts to predict political orientation from Twitter data. Most of the research has mainly focused on the United States, and hence political leaning has been interpreted as mere sympathy with Democrats or Republicans (e.g., Rao et al., 2010; Conover et al., 2011; Gayo-Avello, 2011a; Pennacchiotti & Popescu, 2011a, 2011b; Al Zamal, Liu, & Ruths, 2012; Boutet, Kim, & Yoneki, 2012; Cohen & Ruths, 2013; Volkova, Coppersmith, & Van Dume, 2014). Political orientation in other countries has been studied by Boutet, Kim, and Yoneki (2012) and Barberá (2012), who focused on the United Kingdom and Spain, respectively.

Moreover, such approaches have simplified political orientation into a discrete and binary feature; in other words, they have actually predicted political affiliation. In this regard, just two serious attempts have been made to predict political orientation from Twitter data as a continuous variable – namely, the works by Golbeck and Hansen (2011) and Barberá (2012).

Finally, although precision reported in the literature when predicting political orientation is usually high, greater than 90 percent, Cohen and Ruths (2013) have shown that those values are misleading because datasets overrepresent politically active users. Hence, when using more balanced datasets (i.e., those including "normal users" in addition to politically active ones), precision is much lower: 65 percent.

It must be noted that political leaning of users can be determined not only from the content they produce but also by leveraging information available from their neighbors. Hence, label propagation methods can be useful (e.g., Conover et al., 2011; Gayo-Avello, 2011a; Golbeck & Hansen, 2011; Al Zamal, Liu, & Ruths., 2012; Weber, Garimella, & Batayneh, 2013).

3.4. *Limitations Due to Misinformation and Provenance of Tweets*

There is an additional argument against the simplest approaches to mining opinion from Twitter data: the pitfall of assuming that every tweet is true. In other words, neglecting the fact that wrong information (misinformation) is unavoidable when contents are generated by users, and ignoring that misleading information (disinformation) is not uncommon when discussing politics, and even expected during electoral campaigns.

Fortunately, the topic is attracting attention from the research community, and some promising methods are being developed to face such a challenge. In this regard, there are a number of pioneering works that anyone interested in this subarea should study.

To the best of this author's knowledge, one of the first works regarding the automated analysis of Twitter credibility was conducted by Mendoza, Poblete, and Castillo (2010). In that work, they focused on the way in which information about the 2010 earthquake in Chile spread through Twitter. The authors showed the different spreading patterns of newsworthy information and false rumors, and, hence they set the basis for automatically detecting them in Twitter. Further research along these lines has been published by Castillo, Mendoza, and Poblete (2011, 2013).

With regard to the topic of political disinformation in Twitter, Metaxas and Mustafaraj (2010) were the first to detect and describe a concerted campaign to discredit a candidate using Twitter. They described how a political group used automated accounts to address misleading tweets to Twitter users. Purportedly, those users were expected to spread the disinformation even further. The discovery of "Twitter bombs" was the starting point for a fruitful line of research on the automated analysis of astroturfing and disinformation political campaigns (e.g., Ratkiewicz et al., 2011a, 2011b).

Finally, the report by Mitchell and Hitlin (2013) is crucial to appreciate the limitations of any approach to analyze political opinion in Twitter. First, it clearly shows that Twitter opinion is at odds with public opinion most of the time. Second, it reveals that Twitter opinion is not consistent; that is, sometimes it seems to be more liberal than the population as a whole, while on other occasions it is more conservative. They offer a worrisome conclusion:

> Overall, the reaction to political events on Twitter reflects a combination of the unique profile of active Twitter users and the extent to which events engage different communities and draw the comments of active users. While this provides an interesting look into how communities of interest respond to different circumstances, it does not reliably correlate with the overall reaction of adults nationwide.

3.5. Limitations of Common Approaches to Twitter-based Electoral Forecasting

Electoral forecasting based on Twitter data is affected by all of previous limitations, although to different extents.

For instance, unlike general public opinion polling, elections have a limited set of options (i.e., the candidates), and the implicit question for the public is perfectly clear. Hence, in this regard the "pollster approach" is not particularly problematic. Nevertheless, because Twitter users exhibit different degrees of political engagement, it is unclear how much weight should be assigned to each individual tweet discussing a given candidate. It is still open for discussion whether it should be "one user, one vote," or "one tweet, one vote."

The different sources of bias are also a matter of concern, and it has become an urgent need to correct the data to account for them (e.g., Gayo-Avello, 2011b). These representativeness issues, although challenging, could be tractable provided that user profiling and content-based geolocation are applied. In contrast, self-selection bias, particularly silent majorities, can be a major problem (e.g., Gayo-Avello, 2011b; Mustafaraj et al., 2011).

Another matter of concern is related to the parties to be considered or excluded when collecting the data and making the forecasts. For instance, the forecasts for the 2010 German elections were quite different depending on whether the Pirate Party was being considered or not. In that particular case, it could be somewhat reasonable to exclude the party on the basis that it was not represented in the German parliament. However, there are situations in which previously unrepresented parties get seats; for instance, in the 2014 European Parliament elections, new parties from eighteen different countries got seventy-six seats (10.11 percent of the parliament).

Other limitations, such as those due to the automated content analysis methods or adversarial behaviors, are much more worrisome. Regarding the former, political language exhibits particular features that make it specially difficult for analysis. Adversarial situations such as employing automated accounts,

buying followers, or spreading misleading information are increasingly common during campaigns and present a dire problem for any method approaching
Twitter-based electoral forecasting following a "pollster perspective."

Because of all of these issues, methods based on both Twitter data and
external sources of information such as pre-electoral polls are promising.
Since such approaches would fit a model to data from actual polls, they could
be reasonably immune to the different kinds of bias (even self-selection bias)
and even make unnecessary the application of opinion mining. However, such
methods still need to be put to the test with different elections and for a number
of electoral cycles.

Indeed, one of the major limitations of previous methods to forecast elections from Twitter is, precisely, the way in which their performance was evaluated. First of all, most of the work has been conducted after elections were
held. Second, attention has been mostly paid to whether the method is able to
predict the winner, not to checking the accuracy of the predictions for all of
the parties running for elections. Finally, unnecessary, simplistic (usually random) baselines have been used for comparison instead of others that are more
reasonable, such as incumbency (Metaxas, Mustafaraj, & Gayo-Avello, 2011;
Gayo-Avello, 2013).

4. Implications and Future Work

The importance of public opinion in modern democracies is undeniable, and
efforts to improve the insights about it are welcome. In this regard, mining
social media to ascertain public opinion is the next logical step. After all, social
media in general, and Twitter in particular, provide users with tools to express
their opinions and to organize themselves into communities. It is possible that
political discussion in online media does not fulfill most of the requirements of
the public sphere, but opinionated tweets of political nature are still amenable
to analysis, at least following a "pollster approach."

In fact, such an approach has already produced a relevant number of
research works that provide grounds for cautious optimism. Certainly, most
of such work does not, strictly speaking, deal with public opinion but with
public sentiment on reaction to political events. Still, a few research works
have shown that there may exist a certain correlation between sentiment, as
measured from Twitter, and a number of indices usually obtained by polling. Even so, much more work is needed, since other analyses have reported
that Twitter opinion and public opinion as measured by surveys are often
different.

Furthermore, a concrete application of these techniques, electoral forecast-ing, is still controversial, because, up to now, results from different teams have been mixed and, to some extent, contradictory. Still, recent research seems to prove that tweets about candidates and parties exhibit a subtle predictive power with regard to electoral outcomes. Therefore, Twitter-based electoral forecast-ing is not an unreasonable idea, but further research is needed.

A good deal of the controversy surrounding Twitter-based public opin-ion may be due to the way in which some initial research was conducted and reported. Many of those works blithely ignored the different sources of bias and other issues affecting Twitter, and, on the sole basis of results achieved in single experiments, they claimed tweets had an astounding predictive power. Later results were mixed, and such additional evidence provided a more nuanced picture of Twitter-based nowcasting and forecasting.

Those working on such endeavors must acknowledge, on the one hand, the many challenges they face, such as the difficulties of automated sentiment anal-ysis, in particular regarding political tweets; the need to perform user profiling and geolocation to contend with the demographic biases in Twitter; or the fact that Twitter is an adversarial scenario, and thus both the factuality and prov-enance of tweets must be carefully determined. On the other hand, researchers and practitioners have to recognize the limitations that Twitter imposes – fun-damentally, the self-selection bias that operates at different scales and for dif-ferent topics.

To close this chapter, there are a number of lines of research to which the reader should pay attention.

First of all, in the near term there will be additional efforts to improve Twitter data by removing bias and detecting and filtering misinformation, dis-information, and automated activity. Such methods are unavoidable require-ments to approximate Twitter-based methods to polling techniques.

With regard to new ways to forecast with Twitter data, this author considers that statistical models such as those illustrated by Shi et al. (2012), Lampos (2012), Lampos, Preotiuc-Pietro, and Cohn (2013), Huberty (2013), and Beauchamp (2014) are promising.

Furthermore, this author ventures to suggest a few lines of research that could potentially improve the power of Twitter-based opinion mining. First, it may worth the effort to move beyond sentiment analysis into the formal-ized realm of preferences (e.g., Grandi et al., 2014; cf. Rossi, Venable, & Walsh, 2011). Next, the work by Klimek et al. (2012) on detection of elec-tion irregularities could eventually help to determine whether automated methods are used in Twitter to tamper with the public perception of candi-dates. Furthermore, there have been some efforts to quantify the size of "silent majorities" (Venkataraman, Subbalakshmi, & Chandramouli, 2012), which are a grave consequence of self-selection bias.

Lastly, there are two questions that still remain unanswered: on the one hand, how can survey questions (particularly those that are broad or open-ended) be translated into keywords suitable to collect Twitter data; and, on the other hand, how can the issues comprising the public agenda be ascertained at a greater depth than the available trending topic algorithms are capable of achieving?

Hence, although the Twittersphere's opinion is not public opinion, any attempt to use it as a proxy for the latter is worthy. Notwithstanding, readers are advised to avoid simplistic approaches and direct their efforts to the most needed (although certainly challenging) lines of research summarized in this chapter.

References

Al Zamal, F., Liu, W., & Ruths, D. (2012). Homophily and latent attribute inference: inferring latent attributes of Twitter users from neighbors. In *ICWSM '12* (p. 1). AAAI.

Allport, F. H. (1937). Toward a science of public opinion. *Public Opinion Quarterly*, 1(1), 7–23.

Asur, S., & Huberman, B. A. (2010). Predicting the future with social media. In *Web Intelligence and Intelligent Agent Technology (WI-IAT), 2010 IEEE/WIC/ACM International Conference*, ed. Xiangji Jimmy Huang, Irwin King, Vijay Rahhavan, and Stefan Ruger (vol. 1, pp. 492–9). IEEE.

Bailey, R. W. (2013). *Gay Politics, Urban Politics: Identity and Economics in the Urban Setting*. Columbia University Press.

Bakliwal, A., Foster, J., van der Puil, J., O'Brien, R., Tounsi, L., & Hughes, M. (2013). Sentiment analysis of political tweets: towards an accurate classifier. *NAACL*, 49, 49–58.

Barberá, P. (2012). A new measure of party identification in Twitter: evidence from Spain. In *Proceedings of the 2nd Annual General Conference of EPSA*. European Political Science Association.

Barreto, M. A., & Bozonelos, D. N. (2009). Democrat, Republican, or none of the above? The role of religiosity in Muslim American party identification. *Politics and Religion*, 2(02), 200–29.

Beauchamp, N. (2014). Predicting and interpolating state-level polling using Twitter textual data. Working paper.

Bermingham, A., & Smeaton, A. F. (2011). On using Twitter to monitor political sentiment and predict election results. In *Proceedings of the Workshop on Sentiment Analysis Where AI Meets Psychology (SAAIP), IJCNLP 2011* (pp. 2–10). Asian Federation of Natural Language Processing.

Bollen, J., Mao, H., & Pepe, A. (2010). Determining the public mood state by analysis of microblogging posts. In *Proceedings of the ALIFE XII Conference* (pp. 667–8). ALIFE.

Bollen, J., Mao, H., & Pepe, A. (2011). Modeling public mood and emotion: Twitter sentiment and socio-economic phenomena. In *Proceedings of the Fifth International AAAI Conference on Weblogs and Social Media*. ICWSM.

Borondo, J., Morales, A. J., Losada, J. C., & Benito, R. M. (2012). Characterizing and modeling an electoral campaign in the context of Twitter: 2011 Spanish presidential election as a case study. *Chaos*, 22(2), 023138.

Bourdieu, P. (1979). Public opinion does not exist. *Communication and Class Struggle*, 1, 124–310.

Boutet, A., Kim, H., & Yoneki, E. (2012). What's in your tweets? I know who you supported in the UK 2010 general election. In *Proceedings of the Sixth International AAAI. Conference on Weblogs and Social Media (ICWSM)*.

Bradley, M. M., & Lang, P. J. (1999). Affective norms for English words (ANEW): instruction manual and affective ratings (pp. 1–45). Technical Report C-1, Center for Research in Psychophysiology, University of Florida.

Burnap, P., Rana, O. F., Avis, N., Williams, M., Housley, W., Edwards, A., Morgan, J., & Sloan, L. (forthcoming). Detecting tension in online communities with computational Twitter analysis. *Technological Forecasting and Social Change*.

Caldarelli, G., Chessa, A., Pammolli, F., Pompa, G., Puliga, M., Riccaboni, M., & Riotta, G. (2014). A multi-level geographical study of Italian political elections from Twitter data. *PLOS ONE*, 9(5), e95809.

Campbell, D. E., & Monson, J. Q. (2008). The religion card: gay marriage and the 2004 presidential election. *Public Opinion Quarterly*, 72(3), 399–419.

Carvalho, P., Sarmento, L., Silva, M. J., & de Oliveira, E. (2009). Clues for detecting irony in user-generated contents: oh...!! it's so easy;-). In *Proceedings of the 1st International CIKM Workshop on Topic-Sentiment Analysis for Mass Opinion* (pp. 53–6). ACM.

Castillo, C., Mendoza, M., & Poblete, B. (2011). Information credibility on Twitter. In *Proceedings of the 20th International Conference on the World Wide Web* (pp. 675–84). ACM.

Castillo, C., Mendoza, M., & Poblete, B. (2013). Predicting information credibility in time-sensitive social media. *Internet Research*, 23(5), 560–88.

Ceron, A., Curini, L., Iacus, S. M., & Porro, G. (2013). Every tweet counts? How sentiment analysis of social media can improve our knowledge of citizens' political preferences with an application to Italy and France. *New Media & Society*, 1461444813480466.

Choi, H., & Varian, H. (2012). Predicting the present with Google trends. *Economic Record*, 88(s1), 2–9.

Chu, Z., Gianvecchio, S., Wang, H., & Jajodia, S. (2010). Who is tweeting on Twitter: human, bot, or cyborg? In *Proceedings of the 26th Annual Computer Security Applications Conference* (pp. 21–30). ACM.

Cohen, R., & Ruths, D. (2013). Classifying political orientation on Twitter: It's not easy! In *Proceedings of the 7th International Conference on Weblogs and Social Media*. AAAI.

Conover, M. D., Gonçalves, B., Ratkiewicz, J., Flammini, A., & Menczer, F. (2011). Predicting the political alignment of twitter users. In *Privacy, Security, Risk and Trust (PASSAT), 2011 IEEE Third International Conference on and 2011 IEEE Third International Conference on Social Computing (SocialCom)* (pp. 192–9). IEEE.

Conover, P. J. (1988). Feminists and the gender gap. *Journal of Politics*, 50(04), 985–1010.

DeSipio, L. (1998). *Counting on the Latino Vote: Latinos as a New Electorate.* University of Virginia Press.

Dean, J. (2003). Why the net is not a public sphere. *Constellations*, 10(1), 95–112.

Dean, J. (2013). *Blog Theory: Feedback and Capture in the Circuits of Drive.* John Wiley & Sons.

DiGrazia, J., McKelvey, K., Bollen, J., & Rojas, F. (2013). More tweets, more votes: social media as a quantitative indicator of political behavior. *PLOS ONE*, 8(11), e79449.

Diakopoulos, N. A., & Shamma, D. A. (2010). Characterizing debate performance via aggregated twitter sentiment. In *Proceedings of the SIGCHI Conference on Human Factors in Computing Systems* (pp. 1195–8). ACM.

Esuli, A., & Sebastiani, F. (2006). Sentiwordnet: a publicly available lexical resource for opinion mining. In *Proceedings of LREC* (vol. 6, pp. 417–22).

Freelon, D. (2013). Discourse architecture, ideology, and democratic norms in online political discussion. *New Media & Society*, 1461444813513259.

Freelon, D. G. (2010). Analyzing online political discussion using three models of democratic communication. *New Media & Society*, 12(7), 1172–90.

Gainsborough, J. F. (2001). *Fenced Off: The Suburbanization of American Politics.* Georgetown University Press.

Gayo-Avello, D. (2011a). All liaisons are dangerous when all your friends are known to us. In *Proceedings of the 22nd ACM Conference on Hypertext and Hypermedia* (pp. 171–80). ACM.

Gayo-Avello, D. (2011b). Don't turn social media into another "Literary Digest" poll. *Communications of the ACM*, 54(10), 121–8.

Gayo-Avello, D. (2012). No, you cannot predict elections with Twitter. *Internet Computing, IEEE*, 16(6), 91–4.

Gayo-Avello, D. (2013). A meta-analysis of state-of-the-art electoral prediction from Twitter data. *Social Science Computer Review*, 31(6), 649–79.

Ginsberg, J., Mohebbi, M. H., Patel, R. S., Brammer, L., Smolinski, M. S., & Brilliant, L. (2009). Detecting influenza epidemics using search engine query data. *Nature*, 457(7232), 1012–14.

Glenn, N. D., & Hill, L. (1977). Rural-urban differences in attitudes and behavior in the United States. *Annals of the American Academy of Political and Social Science*, 429(1), 36–50.

Golbeck, J., & Hansen, D. (2011). Computing political preference among Twitter followers. In *Proceedings of the SIGCHI Conference on Human Factors in Computing Systems* (pp. 1105–8). ACM.

Grandi, U., Loreggia, A., Rossi, F., & Saraswat, V. (2014). From sentiment analysis to preference aggregation. In *Proceedings of the 2014 International Symposium on Artificial Intelligence and Mathematics (ISAIM-2014).* AAAI Press.

Green, D. P., Palmquist, B., & Schickler, E. (2004). *Partisan Hearts and Minds: Political Parties and the Social Identities of Voters.* Yale University Press.

Green, J. C., Smidt, C. E., Guth, J. L., & Kellstedt, L. A. (2005). The American religious landscape and the 2004 presidential vote: increased polarization. Paper circulated by Bliss Institute, University of Akron.

Habermas, J. (1991). *The Structural Transformation of the Public Sphere: An Inquiry into a Category of Bourgeois Society*. MIT Press.

Hertzog, M. (1996). *The Lavender Vote: Lesbians, Gay Men, and Bisexuals in American Electoral Politics*. NYU Press.

Huberty, M. E. (2013). Multi-cycle forecasting of congressional elections with social media. In *Proceedings of the 2nd workshop on Politics, Elections and Data* (pp. 23–30). ACM.

Huberty, M. E. (2015). Awaiting the second big data revolution: From digital noise to value creation. *Journal of Industry, Competition and Trade*. Online first article.

Jalalzai, F. (2009). The politics of Muslims in America. *Politics and Religion*, 2(02), 163–99.

Jansen, B. J., Zhang, M., Sobel, K., & Chowdury, A. (2009). Twitter power: tweets as electronic word of mouth. *Journal of the American Society for Information Science and Technology*, 60(11), 2169–88.

Jensen, M. J., & Anstead, N. (2013). Psephological investigations: tweets, votes, and unknown unknowns in the republican nomination process. *Policy & Internet*, 5(2), 161–82.

Jungherr, A., Jürgens, P., & Schoen, H. (2012). Why the Pirate Party won the German election of 2009 or the trouble with predictions: a response to Tumasjan, A., Sprenger, T.O., Sander, P.G., & Welpe, I.M. "Predicting elections with Twitter: what 140 characters reveal about political sentiment." *Social Science Computer Review*, 30(2), 229–34.

Kalampokis, E., Tambouris, E., & Tarabanis, K. (2013). Understanding the predictive power of social media. *Internet Research*, 23(5), 544–59.

Klimek, P., Yegorov, Y., Hanel, R., & Thurner, S. (2012). Statistical detection of systematic election irregularities. *Proceedings of the National Academy of Sciences*, 109(41), 16469–73.

Lampos, V. (2012). On voting intentions inference from Twitter content: a case study on UK 2010 general election. arXiv preprint arXiv:1204.0423.

Lampos, V., De Bie, T., & Cristianini, N. (2010). Flu detector-tracking epidemics on Twitter. In *Machine Learning and Knowledge Discovery in Databases* (pp. 599–602). Springer Berlin Heidelberg.

Lampos, V., Preotiuc-Pietro, D., & Cohn, T. (2013). A user-centric model of voting intention from social media. In *Proceedings of the 51st Annual Meeting of the Association for Computational Linguistics* (pp. 993–1003). Association for Computational Linguistics.

Lansdall-Welfare, T., Lampos, V., & Cristianini, N. (2012). Nowcasting the mood of the nation. *Significance*, 9(4), 26–8.

Laver, M., Benoit, K., & Garry, J. (2003). Extracting policy positions from political texts using words as data. *American Political Science Review*, 97(02), 311–31.

Leighley, J. E., & Nagler, J. (1992). Individual and systemic influences on turnout: who votes? 1984. *Journal of Politics*, 54(03), 718–40.

Livne, A., Simmons, M. P., Adar, E., & Adamic, L. A. (2011). The party is over here: structure and content in the 2010 election. *ICWSM* (July).

Marchetti-Bowick, M., & Chambers, N. (2012). Learning for microblogs with distant supervision: political forecasting with Twitter. In *Proceedings of the 13th*

Conference of the European Chapter of the Association for Computational Linguistics (pp. 603–12). Association for Computational Linguistics.

Mejova, Y. A. (2012). Sentiment analysis within and across social media streams. Ph.D. (doctor of philosophy) thesis, available at http://ir.uiowa.edu/etd/2943.

Mendoza, M., Poblete, B., & Castillo, C. (2010). Twitter under crisis: can we trust what we RT? In *Proceedings of the First Workshop on Social Media Analytics* (pp. 71–79). ACM.

Metaxas, P. T., & Mustafaraj, E. (2010). From obscurity to prominence in minutes: political speech and real-time search. In *Proceedings of Web Science Conference 2010*. ACM.

Metaxas, P. T., & Mustafaraj, E. (2012). Social media and the elections. *Science,* 338(6106), 472–3.

Metaxas, P. T., Mustafaraj, E., & Gayo-Avello, D. (2011). How (not) to predict elections. In *Privacy, Security, Risk and Trust (PASSAT), 2011 IEEE Third International Conference on and 2011 IEEE Third International Conference on Social Computing (SocialCom)* (pp. 165–71). IEEE.

Miller, P. V. (1995). The industry of public opinion. In *Public Opinion and the Communication of Consent*, ed. Theodore L. Glasser and Charles T. Salmon (pp. 105–31). Guilford Press.

Mislove, A., Lehmann, S., Ahn, Y. Y., Onnela, J. P., & Rosenquist, J. N. (2011). Understanding the demographics of Twitter users. *ICWSM*, 11 (5).

Mitchell, A., & Hitlin, P. (2013). Twitter reaction to events often at odds with overall public opinion. Technical Report. Pew Research Center.

Morstatter, F., Pfeffer, J., Liu, H., & Carley, K. M. (2013). Is the sample good enough? Comparing data from Twitter's streaming API with Twitter's firehose. In *Proceedings of ICWSM*. AAAI Press.

Mustafaraj, E., Finn, S., Whitlock, C., & Metaxas, P. T. (2011). Vocal minority versus silent majority: discovering the opinions of the long tail. In *Privacy, Security, Risk and Trust (PASSAT), 2011 IEEE Third International Conference on and 2011 IEEE Third International Conference on Social Computing (SocialCom)* (pp. 103–10). IEEE.

O'Connor, B., Balasubramanyan, R., Routledge, B. R., & Smith, N. A. (2010). From tweets to polls: linking text sentiment to public opinion time series. *ICWSM'10*, 122–9.

Olson, L. R., & Green, J. C. (2006). The religion gap. *PS: Political Science & Politics,* 39(3), 455–9.

Pennacchiotti, M., & Popescu, A. M. (2011a). A machine learning approach to Twitter user classification. In *Proceedings of the Fifth International AAAI Conferences on Weblogs and Social Media* (pp. 281–8). AAAI Press.

Pennacchiotti, M., & Popescu, A. M. (2011b). Democrats, Republicans and Starbucks afficionados: user classification in Twitter. In *Proceedings of the 17th ACM SIGKDD International Conference on Knowledge Discovery and Data Mining* (pp. 430–8). ACM.

Rao, D., Yarowsky, D., Shreevats, A., & Gupta, M. (2010). Classifying latent user attributes in Twitter. In *Proceedings of the 2nd International Workshop on Search and Mining User-Generated Contents* (pp. 37–44). ACM.

Ratkiewicz, J., Conover, M., Meiss, M., Gonçalves, B., Flammini, A., & Menczer, F. (2011a). Detecting and tracking political abuse in social media. In *Proceedings* of the Fifth International AAAI Conferences on Weblogs and Social Media (pp. 297–304). AAAI.

Ratkiewicz, J., Conover, M., Meiss, M., Gonçalves, B., Patil, S., Flammini, A., & Menczer, F. (2011b). Truthy: mapping the spread of astroturf in microblog streams. In *Proceedings of the 20th International Conference Companion on the World Wide Web* (pp. 249–52). ACM.

Reyes, Antonio, Paolo Rosso, and Davide Buscaldi. From humor recognition to irony detection: the figurative language of social media. *Data & Knowledge Engineering* 74 (2012), 1–12.

Rogers, R. (2013). *Foreword: Debanalising Twitter* (vol. 89, pp. ix–xxvi). Peter Lang.

Rossi, F., Venable, K. B., & Walsh, T. (2011). A short introduction to preferences: between artificial intelligence and social choice. *Synthesis Lectures on Artificial Intelligence and Machine Learning*, 5(4), 1–102.

Sang, E. T. K., & Bos, J. (2012). Predicting the 2011 Dutch senate election results with Twitter. In *Proceedings of the Workshop on Semantic Analysis in Social Media* (pp. 53–60). Association for Computational Linguistics.

Sauerzopf, R., & Swanstrom, T. (1999). The urban electorate in presidential elections, 1920–1996. *Urban Affairs Review*, 35(1), 72–91.

Schoen, H., Gayo-Avello, D., Metaxas, P. T., Mustafaraj, E., Strohmaier, M., & Gloor, P. (2013). The power of prediction with social media. *Internet Research*, 23(5), 528–43.

Seltzer, R., Newman, J., & Leighton, M. V. (1997). *Sex as a Political Variable: Women as Candidates and Voters in US Elections*. Lynne Rienner.

Shapiro, R. Y., & Mahajan, H. (1986). Gender differences in policy preferences: a summary of trends from the 1960s to the 1980s. *Public Opinion Quarterly*, 50(1), 42–61.

Sherrill, K. (1996). The political power of lesbians, gays, and bisexuals. *PS: Political Science & Politics*, 29(03), 469–73.

Shi, L., Agarwal, N., Agrawal, A., Garg, R., & Spoelstra, J. (2012). Predicting US primary elections with Twitter. In *Proceedings of Social Network and Social Media Analysis: Methods, Models and Applications (NIPS Workshop), Lake Tahoe, NV, December*, vol. 7.

Signorini, A., Segre, A. M., & Polgreen, P. M. (2011). The use of Twitter to track levels of disease activity and public concern in the US during the influenza A H1N1 pandemic. *PLOS ONE*, 6(5), e19467.

Skoric, M., Poor, N., Achananuparp, P., Lim, E. P., & Jiang, J. (2012). Tweets and votes: a study of the 2011 Singapore general election. In *2012 45th Hawaii International Conference on System Science (HICSS)* (pp. 2583–91). IEEE.

Tam, W. K. (1995). Asians – a monolithic voting bloc? *Political Behavior*, 17(2), 223–49.

Tate, K. (ed.). (1994). *From Protest to Politics: The New Black Voters in American Elections*. Harvard University Press.

Tavares, G., & Faisal, A. (2013). Scaling-laws of human broadcast communication enable distinction between human, corporate and robot twitter users. *PLOS ONE*, 8(7), e65774.

Tufekci, Z. (2014). Big questions for social media big data: representativeness, validity and other methodological pitfalls. In *Proceedings of the Seventh International Conference on Weblogs and Social Media*. AAAI.

Tumasjan, A., Sprenger, T. O., Sandner, P. G., & Welpe, I. M. (2010). Predicting elections with Twitter: what 140 characters reveal about political sentiment. *ICWSM*, 10, 178–85.

Turney, P. D. (2002). Thumbs up or thumbs down? Semantic orientation applied to unsupervised classification of reviews. In *Proceedings of the 40th Annual Meeting on Association for Computational Linguistics* (pp. 417–424). Association for Computational Linguistics.

Van Dijck, J. (2013). *The Culture of Connectivity: A Critical History of Social Media*. Oxford University Press.

Venkataraman, M., Subbalakshmi, K. P., & Chandramouli, R. (2012, May). Measuring and quantifying the silent majority on the Internet. In *Sarnoff Symposium (SARNOFF), 2012 35th IEEE* (pp. 1–5). IEEE.

Volkova, S., Coppersmith, G., & Van Dume, B. (2014). Inferring user political preferences from streaming communications. In *Proceedings of the Association for Computational Linguistics (ACL)*. Association for Computational Linguistics.

Walks, R. A. (2006). The causes of city-suburban political polarization? A Canadian case study. *Annals of the Association of American Geographers*, 96(2), 390–414.

Wattenberg, Martin P. (2008). *Is Voting for Young People? With a Postscript on Citizen Engagement*. Longman.

Weber, I., Garimella, V. R. K., & Batayneh, A. (2013). Secular vs. Islamist polarization in Egypt on Twitter. In *Proceedings of the 2013 IEEE/ACM International Conference on Advances in Social Networks Analysis and Mining* (pp. 290–7). ACM.

Wilson, T., Wiebe, J., & Hoffmann, P. (2005). Recognizing contextual polarity in phrase-level sentiment analysis. In *Proceedings of the Conference on Human Language Technology and Empirical Methods in Natural Language Processing* (pp. 347–54). Association for Computational Linguistics.

Wolfinger, R. E. (1980). *Who Votes?* (Vol. 22). Yale University Press.

Wong, F. M. F., Sen, S., & Chiang, M. (2012). Why watching movie tweets won't tell the whole story? In *Proceedings of the 2012 ACM Workshop on Workshop on Online Social Networks* (pp. 61–6). ACM.

Yu, B., Kaufmann, S., & Diermeier, D. (2008). Exploring the characteristics of opinion expressions for political opinion classification. In *Proceedings of the 2008 International Conference on Digital Government Research* (pp. 82–91). Digital Government Society of North America.

Zhang, C. M., & Paxson, V. (2011, January). Detecting and analyzing automated activity on Twitter. In *Passive and Active Measurement*, ed. Neil Spring and George F. Riley (pp. 102–11). Springer Berlin Heidelberg.

3

Socioeconomic Indicators

Huina Mao

Twitter has been widely used for human behavior research with its applications in public opinion mining (cf. Chapter 3), studying well-being (cf. Chapter 4), disease monitoring (cf. Chapter 5), and disaster mapping (cf. Chapter 6). In this chapter, we review existing work on using Twitter data to measure socioeconomic indicators, including unemployment rate, consumer confidence, social mood, investor sentiment, and financial markets. Moreover, to complement research with Twitter data, we use several examples to illustrate the use of other large-scale data sources (e.g., web search queries, mobile phone calls) for socioeconomic measurement and prediction. At the end, we discuss challenges with existing research and identify several directions for future work.

1. Introduction

There has been considerable success in leveraging large-scale social media data at the intersection of social sciences and computational sciences with myriad applications in socioeconomic measurement and prediction.

An early study (Antweiler & Frank, 2004) finds that the message volume of stock message boards on Yahoo! Finance[1] and Raging Bull[2] can predict market volatility, and disagreement among posted messages is related to high trading volume. Public mood indicators extracted from social networks such as Facebook (Karabulut, 2011), LiveJournal (Gilbert & Karahalios, 2010), and Twitter (Bollen, Mao, & Zeng, 2011) can predict stock market fluctuations. Zhang, Fuehres, and Gloor (2010) study the correlation between emotional

---

[1] http://finance.yahoo.com/mb/.
[2] http://ragingbull.com/.

tweets and financial market indicators. They find that the percentage of emotional tweets is negatively correlated with Dow Jones, NASDAQ, and Standard and Poor's (S&P) 500 values, but positively correlated with Volatility Index (VIX). Bollen, Mao, and Zeng (2011) develop a multidimensional mood analysis model that can track Twitter mood in six dimensions (i.e., calm, alert, sure, vital, kind, and happy) and find that Twitter calmness has significant predictive power on daily Dow Jones Industrial Average (DJIA) price changes. Mao et al. (2012) investigate the relation between daily number of stock tweets (i.e., those containing individual stock ticker names) and S&P 500 indicators (prices and traded volume) and find significant correlation at three different levels: the overall stock market, industry sector, and individual stocks. Also, adding Twitter data can improve prediction of the S&P 500 closing price at the stock market level. Asur and Huberman (2010) provide a demonstration that Twitter content and sentiment can be used to forecast box-office revenues of movies. Similarly, Gruhl et al. (2005) show that online chatter volume can predict book sales. O'Connor et al. (2010) report a high correlation between sentiment word frequency in Twitter messages versus consumer confidence and political opinions.

In this chapter, we focus on reviewing recent socioeconomic research with Twitter data. We also briefly discuss the potential of other large-scale data sources for this research. Many facets of our life are recorded by various types of large-scale data, including social media, search engines, phone records, emails, Global Positioning System (GPS) data, shopping records, and electronic sensors. Integrating social media data with other big data sources can enhance our deep understanding of human behavior and economic activities.

While social media data capture information-*sharing* behavior, web search queries reveal people's information-*seeking* behavior. Several studies of web search data have shown that people's online search behavior is related to and even predictive of economic activity. Ettredge, Gerdes, and Karuga (2005) find that job-related searches are positively correlated to official unemployment statistics. Google search queries can predict contemporaneous (or "nowcasting") economic indicators, such as car sales, unemployment claims, travel planning, and consumer confidence (Choi & Varian, 2011). Da, Engelberand, and Gao (2011) use changes of Google search volume of stock ticker names as a proxy of investor attention, which can predict short-term stock price movements. Preis et al. (2012) develop a "future orientation index" based on a nation's online volume of search queries for the next year's numeral date, such as searches for "2014" in the year 2013 relative to searches for "2012" in the same year. They find gross domestic product (GDP) per capita is correlated with propensity for a forward-looking attitude as measured by the volume of Google searches.

Compared to social media, mobile phone usage continues to increase rapidly in low-income areas where information infrastructure is lacking. With rising usership, mobile phone call data are more informative and less biased by wealth than the web data. In recent years, phone call data are increasingly leveraged by computational science researchers to study social and economic phenomena. Blondel et al. (2008) distinguish the Flemish and French language communities using Belgian mobile phone network data that pertain to 2.6 million customers, a result that may support future efforts to provide aid that is sensitive to regional, socioeconomic, cultural, and linguistic distinctions. Eagle, Macy, and Claxton (2010) analyze UK national phone communication data, quantify the level of communication diversity of communities, and report a significant correlation between communication diversity and people's economic prosperity. This finding supports the theoretical assumption that heterogeneous, instead of highly clustered, social ties may create the opportunities of social and economic prospects from outside groups (Newman, 2003; Page, 2007).

In addition, satellite imagery is another powerful data source for scientific research. From large-scale satellite imagery data, Graesser et al. (2012) and Vatsavai (2013) detect informal settlements (i.e., unplanned and unauthorized homes) based on their unique spatial characteristics. The integration of satellite data with human-generated social data can provide an even more comprehensive and detailed perspective on a variety of socioeconomic phenomena, and thus a fertile environment for future computational social science research (Lazer et al., 2009).

This line of research suggests that it is feasible to construct new measures of socioeconomic indicators from massive amounts of data generated from disparate sources such as social media, search engines, cell phones, satellites, and electronic sensors. These new sources of data are often referred to as big data. Compared to traditional surveys and official records, big data have the advantages of providing measurements in real time, at a large scale, and at a low cost. Tracking socioeconomic indicators efficiently can improve government efficiency and inform economic policy making.

The rest of this chapter is organized as follows. In Section 2, we survey existing work on using Twitter data to measure socioeconomic indicators, including unemployment rate, consumer confidence, investor sentiment, and stock market activity. Section 3 briefly reviews examples of measuring socioeconomic indicators with search engine and mobile phone data. Finally, we discuss limitations and challenges of measuring socioeconomic indicators from big data and identify some directions for future research.

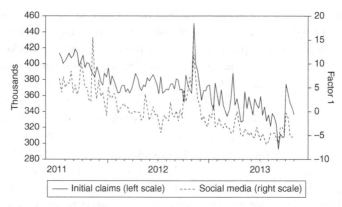

Figure 3.1. Official initial claims for unemployment insurance (left scale, revised data, seasonally adjusted) and the social media factor 1 (right scale). Antenucci et al. (2014).

2. Mining Twitter for Socioeconomic Indicators

Twitter provides an enormous amount of information that has been extensively used for socioeconomic measurements. Here we summarize a series of studies that use Twitter data to measure and predict unemployment rate, consumer confidence, investor sentiment, and financial market activity.

2.1. Unemployment Rate

Unemployment rate is a key indicator of labor market that can help policy makers understand the health of the economy and make informed policy decisions to address labor issues. The official statistics of U.S. unemployment insurance (UI) claims are reported by the Department of Labor on a weekly basis.[3]

A recent work by Antenucci et al. (2014) creates the University of Michigan Social Media Job Loss Index based on principal component analysis of signals derived from tweets containing phrases such as "lost my job," "fired," and "downsized." Figure 3.1 shows time series of official initial claims for unemployment insurance and the first factor from the Twitter job loss and unemployment signals. These two indexes have similar trend and some overlapping spikes. However, they are not perfectly correlated, potentially because they capture different information. As a matter of fact, the social media index is found to be more accurate in predicting *revised* unemployment claims than the

---

[3] http://www.dol.gov/opa/media/press/eta/ui/current.htm.

original number reported one week earlier. This finding suggests that social media may capture the information about the *true* status of the labor market that is not accounted in a timely manner by the original unemployment claims.

2.2. *Consumer Confidence*

The consumer confidence index reveals consumers' attitude and outlook about the overall economic status in a country and their own financial situation. How confident people feel highly influences their economic decision making. In good times, people are confident and prone to spend and purchase. But in bad times, people are lacking confidence, so they hesitate to spend. Therefore, consumer confidence is considered an important indicator of economic trends. Traditional consumer confidence measurements rely on surveys, such as the Michigan Consumer Confidence Index[4] and the Gallup Economic Confidence Index.[5] However, surveys are subject to many disadvantages: small-scale samples, low-frequency updates, and delayed release. In contrast, Twitter is large scale and real time and can thus be used to track consumer confidence at a finer and timelier scale.

O'Connor et al. (2010) select tweets containing keywords such as "jobs," "job," and "economy" and apply a positive/negative lexicon called OpinionFinder[6] to compute sentiment scores x_t on day t according to Equation 3.1. So, daily sentiment score is the ratio of positive versus negative tweets on the topic.

$$x_t = \frac{count_t \ (pos. \ word \wedge topic \ word)}{count_t \ (neg. \ word \wedge topic \ word)} = \frac{p \ (pos. \ word \mid topic \ word, t)}{p \ (neg. \ word \mid topic \ word)} \quad (3.1)$$

By comparing the Twitter sentiment ratio with U.S. consumer confidence surveys – the Michigan Index of Consumer Sentiment (ICS) and the Gallup Economic Confidence Index – they find a significant positive correlation, as shown in Figure 3.2. Moreover, cross-correlation analysis in O'Connor et al. (2010) indicates that a change of Twitter sentiment *leads* the poll-based confidence.

Furthermore, research efforts are extended to measure the consumer confidence index in European countries. Daas and Puts (2014) have found that changes of sentiment in Dutch public social media messages (especially

---

[4] http://www.sca.isr.umich.edu/.
[5] http://www.gallup.com/poll/122840/gallup-daily-economic-indexes.aspx.
[6] http://www.cs.pitt.edu/mpqa.

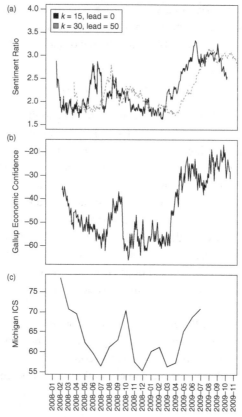

Figure 3.2. Twitter sentiment ratio and consumer confidence surveys. Sentiment information captures broad trends in the survey data. From Tweets to Polls: Linking Text Sentiment to Public Opinion Time Series. O'Connor, B., Balasubramanyan, R., Routledge, B. R., and Smith, N. A. In *Proceedings of the International Conference on Weblogs and Social Media*, Figure 6, page 126, © 2010. Association for the Advancement of Artificial Intelligence.

Facebook) are highly correlated with changes in official consumer confidence, with Pearson correlation coefficient $r > 0.8$. Figure 3.3 shows social media sentiment data aggregated at different time levels – daily, weekly, and monthly – and the official consumer confidence for the same period. A cointegration test indicates that both official consumer confidence and social media sentiment are driven by the same underlying cause, and a Granger-causality test shows that changes of consumer confidence precede changes of social media sentiment. In other words, consumer confidence reacts to the underlying driver faster than social media, which is opposite to the finding of O'Connor et al. (2010), where

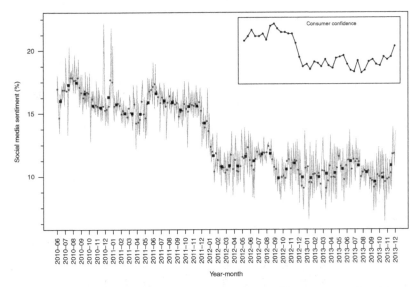

Figure 3.3. Development of daily, weekly, and monthly aggregates of social media sentiment from June 2010 until November 2013, in solid, dotted, and square dashed lines, respectively. In the insert, the development of consumer confidence is shown for the same period.
Daas & Puts (2014).

Twitter *leads* polls. Future work is needed to test further the lead/lag relation between surveys and social media.

2.3. *Social Mood*

Human emotions can profoundly affect individual behavior and decision making. By extension, social mood may influence our economy at the collective level.

Zhang, Fuehres, and Gloor (2010) measure collective mood based on the number of tweets containing emotional words, such as "hope," "fear," "worry," and "happy," and then correlate this with stock market indicators. They find that the emotional tweet percentage – the ratio of emotional tweets to total tweet volume on the same day – displays significant negative correlation to the Dow Jones Industrial Average (DJIA), NASDAQ, and the S&P 500, but positive correlation to VIX (or the "fear index"). The absolute value of correlation coefficient r ranges from 0.2 to 0.4. Figure 3.4 shows the negative correlation between DJIA and the three-day mean of "hope + fear + worry" percentage.

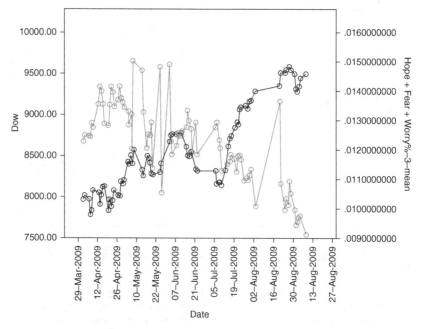

Figure 3.4. Correlation between "hope + fear + worry%-3-mean" and the
Dow Jones Industrial Average. Reprinted from *Social and Behavioral
Sciences*, Zhang, X., Fuehres, H., Gloor, P., Predicting stock market indicators through Twitter: "I hope it is not as bad as I fear." pp. 55–62, Copyright
(2010), with permission from Elsevier.

This observation implies that under economic uncertainty, people tend to use
more emotional words such as "hope," "fear," and "worry."

To test further whether social mood can impact our economy, Bollen, Mao,
and Zeng (2011) study the dynamic properties of public mood states from
Twitter updates and their relations to a variety of socioeconomic phenomena. The authors develop a multidimensional mood analysis method, named
Google Profile of Mood States (GPOMS), to track public mood from Twitter
in six dimensions, including *calm, alert, sure, vital, kind,* and *happy.* They
find that Twitter *calmness* has predictive information with respect to short-term
stock market returns. Figure 3.5 plots time series of Twitter calmness against
daily DJIA price changes, which are delayed by a lag of three days. In other
words, the increase (or decrease) of Twitter mood is followed by increase (or
decrease) of stock market prices.

Bollen, Mao, and Zeng (2011) further conduct Granger-causality analysis to test whether the Twitter mood time series predicts stock market activity. Results are shown in Table 3.1. It can be seen that Twitter *calmness* has

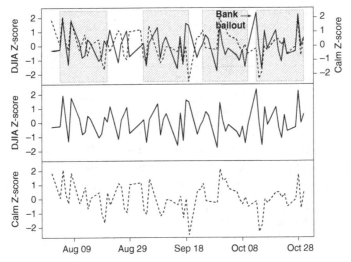

Figure 3.5. Three graphs plotting Twitter calmness against daily DJIA price changes.

The top graph shows the overlap of the day-to-day difference of DJIA values (black: $\mathbb{Z}_{D_t}$) with the GPOMS' Calm time series (gray: $\mathbb{Z}_{X_t}$) that has been lagged by three days. Where the two lines overlap, the Calm time series predicts changes in the DJIA closing values that occur three days later. Areas of significant congruence are marked by a gray background. The middle and bottom graphs show the separate DJIA and GPOMS' Calm time series.

Bollen, Mao, & Zeng (2011).

the most significant Granger-causal relation with DJIA, while the other four mood dimensions of GPOMS are not predictive of the changes in the stock market, and neither is the OpinionFinder time series.[7] In addition to linear Granger-causality analysis, a nonlinear model – Self-organizing Fuzzy Neutral Network – has been applied to predict stock price changes with Twitter mood, which improves the prediction accuracy.

Bollen, Mao, and Zeng (2011) is considered one of the pioneering studies on using Twitter mood to predict the financial market and motivates an increasing amount of research work on this topic. In particular, people are interested in measuring *investor* sentiment from Twitter and testing its prediction on different levels: the overall stock market and individual stocks.

---

[7] OpinionFinder (OF), http://mpqa.cs.pitt.edu/opinionfinder/, is a publicly available software package for sentiment analysis that can be applied to determine positive and negative polarity.

Table 3.1. Statistical significance (p-values) of bivariate Granger-causality correlation between moods and DJIA in period February 28, 2008 to November 3, 2008

Lag	OF	Calm	Alert	Sure	Vital	Kind	Happy
1 day	0.085*	0.272	0.952	0.648	0.120	0.848	0.388
2 days	0.268	0.013**	0.973	0.811	0.369	0.991	0.7061
3 days	0.436	0.022**	0.981	0.349	0.418	0.991	0.723
4 days	0.218	0.030**	0.998	0.415	0.475	0.989	0.750
5 days	0.300	0.036**	0.989	0.544	0.553	0.996	0.173
6 days	0.446	0.065**	0.996	0.691	0.682	0.994	0.081*
7 days	0.620	0.157	0.999	0.381	0.713	0.999	0.150

Note: ** p-value < 0.05, * p-value < 0.01.
Source: Bollen, Mao, and Zeng (2011).

2.4. Investor Sentiment

Investor sentiment is a specific indicator that measures how investors feel about near-term prospects for the stock market. Investor sentiment can cause short-term price changes: bullish sentiment tends to drive more investors to buy, thereby causing prices to increase. On the contrary, bearish sentiment drives more investors to sell, thereby causing prices to decrease. Also, investor sentiment can be used as a contrarian indicator – when the majority buy or sell, it is time to take the opposite action. Therefore, investor sentiment is an important market indicator for traders and investors.

Oh and Sheng (2011) propose a method to analyze investor sentiment from tweets with *cashtags*, that is, the dollar sign ($) followed by the ticker symbols, as in $MSFT, $GOOG, and $AAPL. They first manually annotate 7,109 tweets into three classes – bullish, bearish, and neutral – and then train a machine learning classifier to classify out-of-sample tweets automatically. According to Equation 3.2, the Twitter bullishness score is calculated for each stock ticker on each day.

$$\textit{Bullishness Index} = \ln \frac{\left[1 + M^{BULL}\right]}{\left[1 + M^{BEAR}\right]} \qquad (3.2)$$

where M^{BULL} and M^{BEAR} are the total bullish and bearish tweets, respectively. This index is predictive of the future stock price movement in terms of both simple and adjusted stock returns. This finding supports the investor sentiment hypothesis in behavioral finance: irrationality/sentiment can influence stock market prices. In addition, Oh and Sheng (2011) find that bearish sentiment has a stronger predictive power on stock prices as compared to bullish sentiment. The reason may be that wishful thinking can cause an inflated number of bullish tweets and reduce its predictive accuracy. Wishful thinking refers to a psychological phenomenon: people tend to predict positive outcomes to be more likely than negative outcomes. Overall, the authors show that Twitter does contain valuable information about the stock market, and they support evidence for financial theory testing.

Even though machine learning classifiers have shown considerable promise in measuring investor sentiment, they suffer from measurement and classification errors. According to Das and Chen (2007), Pang and Lee (2008), and Oh and Sheng (2011), a machine learning classification accuracy of 60 to 70 percent is considered acceptable in sentiment analysis.

Mao, Counts, and Bollen (2014) introduce a simple, direct, and unambiguous indicator of investor sentiment by examining finance-related key term frequencies (i.e., "bullish" and "bearish") in Twitter updates. Since "bullish" and "bearish" are very financial-oriented terms and reveal investors' attitude and outlook toward the market, the authors used them to construct a daily investor sentiment index. They define a tweet as bullish if it contains the term "bullish" and bearish if it contains the term "bearish." Over the study period of 2010 to 2012 (in total, 1,091 days), 0.31 million bullish and bearish tweets were obtained. The daily Twitter bullishness index is aggregated based on Equation 3.3.

$$B_t = \ln\left(\frac{1+\|B_t\|}{1+\|R_t\|}\right) \tag{3.3}$$

where B_t and R_t denote the sets of bullish and bearish tweets on day t, respectively. Figure 3.6 shows bullish and bearish tweet volume. Clearly, a weekly pattern can be observed from the autocorrelation and Fast Fourier Transform analysis: there are high tweet volumes during trading days (weekdays), a peak on Tuesday and Thursday, and lower volumes during nontrading days (weekends).

Mao, Counts, and Bollen (2014) apply the Vector Autoregression (VAR) framework[8] to examine whether Twitter bullishness has predictive value with respect to stock market returns. For robustness, the authors test the prediction of Twitter bullishness on a variety of stock market indexes, including the

---

[8]   VAR quantifies the interdependencies among multivariate time series and is widely used to estimate the predictability of indicators in finance.

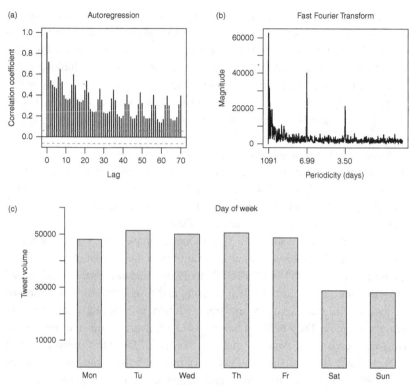

Figure 3.6. Bullish and bearish tweet volume over days of week.
Mao, Counts, & Bollen (2014).

DJIA, S&P 500, large-cap Russell 1000, and small-cap Russell 2000. In the regression model – along with other existing predictors, including calendar, trading volume, VIX, and the survey-based investor sentiment – the Daily Sentiment Index (DSI) is controlled in prediction analysis. Table 3.2 reports the regression coefficient estimates and associated p-values. Each coefficient indicates the impact of one standard deviation increase in Twitter bullishness on daily returns in basis points (1 basis point equals (bps) 0.01 percent of a daily return).

The authors find that one standard deviation increase of Twitter bullishness on day t-1 is followed by 12.56 basis points (bps) increase in DJIA returns on the following day t. This impact is statistically and economically significant. Similar predictive results are obtained for SP 500, Russell 1000, and Russell 2000. Within one week, a reversal sign is observed in Table 3.2. This

Table 3.2. Predicting daily stock returns of Dow Jones, S&P 500, Russell 1000, and Russell 2000 using Twitter bullishness

Bullishness lag	DJIA		S&P 500		Russell 1000		Russell 2000	
	Coeff.	*p*-value	Coeff.	*p*-value	Coeff.	*p*-value	Coeff.	*p*-value
1	12.56	0.01***	10.98	0.05**	10.72	0.05**	11.02	0.05**
2	2.27	0.67	2.61	0.65	2.46	0.67	2.66	0.65
3	2.18	0.69	3.69	0.53	4.037	0.48	4.58	0.43
4	−7.81	0.15	−8.10	0.16	−9.99	0.08*	−10.28	0.08*
5	−1.12	0.80	−1.28	0.79	−1.35	0.77	−1.37	0.78

Note: *** $p \leq 0.001$, ** $p \leq 0.05$, * $p \leq 0.01$.

may provide support to the investor sentiment model proposed by Long et al. (1990), which claims that sentiment or irrationality can drive the asset price to deviate from its fundamental value temporarily, but will reverse to the mean in the long run.

Moreover, Mao, Counts, and Bollen (2014) also compare Twitter bullishness to a survey-based investor sentiment measurement, the Daily Sentiment Index (DSI), for their contemporaneous correlations and predictive effect on stock returns. The Pearson correlation coefficient between DSI and Twitter bullishness is $r = 30$ ($p \ll 0.01$), indicating a positive but not strong correlation. In the prediction, it has been found that a one-standard-deviation increase in DSI is followed by only a 2.26 bps increase of daily Dow returns, which is not significant. So, the investor sentiment measured from Twitter is related to but different from the investor sentiment reported by surveys. The former can have larger financial predictive effects than the latter. Therefore, tracking socioeconomic indicators from Twitter may not only be more efficient than surveys, but also may capture more useful information.

2.5. Twitter Network Features and Financial Markets

Most of existing work as shown in the preceding sections analyze the sentiment of tweets and test its prediction of the stock market. A limited amount of work has considered social network features as a predictor. Here we discuss two studies that attempt to incorporate network features for financial prediction.

First, Ruiz et al. (2012) represent tweets as a graph and construct graph features that are correlated with stock trading volume and prices. Tweets containing stock ticker names and company names are selected for analysis. Figure 3.7 shows the tweet graph schema.

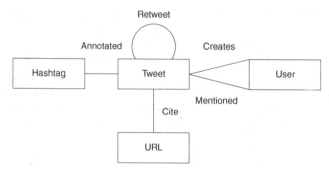

Figure 3.7. Graph schema.
Ruiz et al. (2012).

Graph nodes can be the tweets themselves, users either who post the tweets or are mentioned in the tweets, as well as the hashtags and URLs included in the tweets. The edges in this graph are retweets (between two tweets), authorship (between a tweet and its author), hashtag presence (between a hashtag and the tweets that contain it), URL presence (between a URL and the tweets that contain it), and so on. The graph features include the number of nodes (NUM-NODES), number of edges (NUM-EDGES), number of components (NUM-CMP), diameter, PageRank, and degrees. Each tweet graph is constrained to a stock and a specific time interval. Then, they apply cross-correlation analysis to estimate the relation of Twitter graph features with respect to stock prices and trading volume.

Figure 3.8a shows that NUM-CMP (the number of connected components) and NUM-NODES (the number of nodes) have the strongest correlation with traded volume. Even though the correlation with stock prices is weaker (see Figure 3.8b) than with the traded volume, adding the feature of NUM-CMP into a trading model can improve profits, which significantly outperforms baseline strategies (namely, random, fixed, and autoregression models without considering network features).

Second, Sul, Dennis, and Yuan (2014) study the relation between Twitter emotional valence about a certain company and its abnormal stock returns by adding an additional factor: the number of followers. The number of followers is considered a proxy for the speed of information diffusion. In other words, tweets posted by users with a large number of followers can disseminate more rapidly than those with few followers.

The Harvard IV-dictionary[9] is used to determine the emotional valence of tweets including a stock ticker name. The dictionary includes positive

---

[9]   http://www.wjh.harvard.edu/inquirer/.

(a)

Feature	Lag [days]						
	−3	−2	−1	0	+1	+2	+3
NUM-CMP	0.09	0.11	0.21	0.52	0.33	0.16	0.10
TID	0.09	0.10	0.19	0.49	0.31	0.15	0.09
UID	0.09	0.11	0.21	0.49	0.31	0.15	0.10
NUM-NODES	0.09	0.10	0.20	0.49	0.31	0.15	0.09
NUM-EDGES	0.09	0.09	0.18	0.45	0.29	0.14	0.09

(b)

Feature	Lag [days]						
	−3	−2	−1	0	+1	+2	+3
NUM-CMP	0.08	0.09	0.10	0.13	0.07	0.07	0.07
NUM-NODES	0.07	0.09	0.10	0.11	0.08	0.07	0.07
TID	0.06	0.08	0.07	0.10	0.07	0.08	0.08
UID	0.07	0.08	0.08	0.10	0.07	0.08	0.07
NUM-EDGES	0.07	0.08	0.09	0.10	0.08	0.07	0.06

Figure 3.8. Cross-correlation coefficient of Twitter graph features and stock prices and volume.
Ruiz et al. (2012).

and negative words. The occurrence of positive or negative words in a tweet indicates the positive or negative valence of this tweet. The valence score is aggregated for each stock at each day in three forms shown as in Equation 3.4.

$$valence = \begin{cases} neg1 = \dfrac{N}{T} \\ pos1 = \dfrac{P-N}{P=N} \\ pos2 = \log\left(\dfrac{1+P}{1+N}\right) \end{cases} \tag{3.4}$$

With both factors – tweet valence and number of followers – obtained, the authors find that, firstly, Twitter emotional valence has a significant relation with stock returns; and secondly, tweets from users with a large number of followers (more than the median) have a stronger impact on contemporaneous returns on the same day, but lower predictability on future returns. In contrast, tweets from users with a smaller number of followers (fewer than the median) have a stronger predictability on returns. The results may be explained by the speed of information dissemination. Tweets posted by Twitter users who have a large number of followers are more likely to spread rapidly and thus can be incorporated into market prices immediately. On the other hand, few followers means slow dissemination rate, and thus it will take longer time for stock prices to react to such information.

In summary, studies in Ruiz et al. (2012) and Sul, Dennis, and Yuan (2014) suggest the importance of social network features for studying the relation between human behavior and economy.

3. The Applications of Other Big Data Sources in Economic Research

In addition to social media data, other big data sources, such as search engine and mobile phone data, are leveraged for economic and financial research.

3.1. *Search Volume Data, Financial Market, and GDP*

Google is the largest search engine in the world. Google Trends[10] is a free service that provides weekly search volume data from January 2004 to the present for any given query. Search queries can be filtered by categories (e.g., finance, food, or arts), geography (e.g., worldwide, countries, or states), dates, and search types (e.g., websites, images, and news).

Based on the assumption that searching reveals attention (i.e., when you search something, undoubtedly you pay attention to it), Da, Engelberand, and Gao (2011) propose to measure investor attention directly based on search queries for stock ticker names. Their results have shown, firstly, that there is a positive but low correlation between Google search volume and alternative attention measures. In other words, Google and traditional attention measures are different. Secondly, they find that Google search volume is likely to capture the attention of individual or retail investors.

In a following work, Da, Engelberand, and Goa (2015) construct a Financial and Economic Attitudes Revealed by Search (FEARS) index based on Google search queries for negative economic terms, such as "recession," "unemployment," and "bankruptcy." The FEARS index is found to predict short-term return reversals and temporary increases in volatility, which supports theories of investor sentiment. Therefore, the FEARS index is considered a new measure of investor sentiment.

Moreover, web search queries are used to study macroeconomic indicators, such as GDP. Preis et al. (2012) develop a "future orientation index" based on a nation's online volume of search queries for the next year's numeral date, such as searches for "2010" in the year 2009 relative to searches for "2008" in the same year. They find that a nation's GDP per capita is correlated with their forward-looking attitude as measured by the volume of Google searches

---

[10] http://www.google.com/trends/.

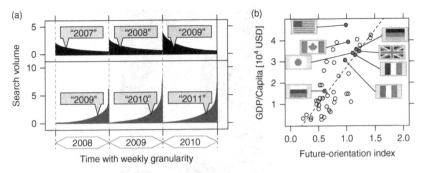

Figure 3.9. Google future orientation index and its correlation with per capita GDP. Reprinted by permission from Macmillan Publishers Ltd: Scientific Reports, 2, Preis, T., Moat, H. S., Stanley, H. E., and Bishop, S. R. Quantifying the advantage of looking forward, (2012). 350.

(see Figure 3.9). However, this research does not show any causal support for the relation between GDP and future orientation; finding such a relation will require future research.

3.2. *Phone Communication Data and Economic Development*

Eagle, Macy, and Claxton (2010) propose a novel method to quantify social diversity based on a phone call network in the UK and study the relation between communication diversity and economic development. The diversity is measured as a function of Shannon entropy. High diversity indicates that a resident communicates with his or her social ties more equally. The authors find that the social network diversity and the socioeconomic well-being of communities (represented by the UK government's Index of Multiple Deprivation) have a strong correlation ($r = 0.73$; see Figure 3.10b). In other words, the communities with higher diversity tend to have a better socioeconomic status (see Figure 3.10).

This research is consistent with social science theories that claim heterogeneous social ties may create the opportunities of social and economic prospects (Newman, 2003; Page, 2007), which inspire future research to investigate the causal mechanisms between social network diversity and economic development.

4. Challenges and Future Research

In this chapter, we have shown that myriad results in computational social science now demonstrate the power of large-scale data and advanced analytics to uncover meaningful correlations and patterns in socioeconomic environments.

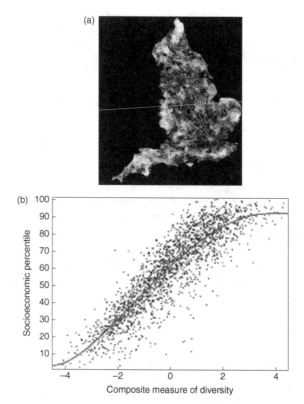

Figure 3.10. Economic development and network diversity.
(a) An image of regional communication diversity and socioeconomic
ranking (represented from light gray to black) for the UK.
(b) The relation between social network diversity and socioeconomic rank.
Eagle, Macy, & Claxton (2010).

People's information sharing, information seeking, and social communication
behaviors revealed from social media, search engines, and mobile phones are
correlated with socioeconomic indicators such as unemployment rate, consumer
confidence, financial markets, and GDP. But the objective of this research is
not to *replicate*, but to *complement* and *improve* administrative socioeconomic
statistics. Measurements with Twitter and other large-scale data sources are
fundamentally different from traditional surveys and official records. Future
research is needed to understand similarities and differences of the socioeconomic statistics derived from traditional surveys and social media data.

Overall, Twitter, which generates unprecedented large-scale data in real
time and at finer granularity, provides us with new opportunities to better

understand and even predict socioeconomic phenomena. However, there are also many limitations and challenges in this research.

First, much of the literature reviewed in this chapter is essentially explorative in nature, that is, it attempts to uncover patterns and regularities without the benefit of a predefined hypothesis, theoretical framework, or research question. However, although two variables can be found to be highly correlated, this does not imply they are causative of each other, nor that they are actually related to each other. In fact, the expression "correlation does not imply causation" is often leveled as a criticism of data-driven, explorative science methods that are focused on establishing correlations between variables measured in a post-hoc fashion from existing data. Scientific hypothesis testing and experimental design can help identify causal relationships. Understanding the underlying mechanisms that may drive the observed correlations allows deduction and prediction beyond observables in the data themselves.

Second, the access to social media is very limited in low-income areas where the information infrastructure is immature. According to the 2013 report of the International Telecommunication Union,[11] only 16 percent of people use the Internet in Africa. The low Twitter usage generates a limited amount of data for research to improve traditional socioeconomic statistics in low-income areas where socioeconomic statistics are scarce. In contrast to social media, the usage of mobile phone is universal and generates a valuable and less wealth-biased data source for us to study economic development patterns. Recent work by Eagle, Macy, and Claxton (2010) – observing a strong correlation between communication diversity measured from phone call networks and the socioeconomic well-being of the communities in the UK – lays the groundwork for future research on low-income areas where there is dearth of official socioeconomic statistics due to the poor information infrastructure. Big data can provide more valuable information in measuring what is *unknown* or *hard to measure*.

Third, using social media and search engine data to construct social, economic, and health indicators has raised some criticisms in the scientific community recently (Lazer et al., 2014). The criticisms include lack of transparency and replicability. In the recent half-decade, there is a significantly increasing amount of research work that extract interesting variables from big data and uncover relation to socioeconomic phenomena. Future efforts should be made to increase the transparency and replicability of big data research.

---

[11] http://www.itu.int/en/ITU-D/Statistics/Pages/publications/mis2013.aspx.

References

Antenucci, D., Cafarella, M., Levenstein, M. C., Ré, C., and Shapiro, M. D. (2014). *Using Social Media to Measure Labor Market Flows*. National Bureau of Economic Research.

Antweiler, W., and Frank, M. Z. (2004, June). Is all that talk just noise? The information content of Internet stock message boards. *Journal of Finance*, 59(3), 1259–94.

Asur, S., and Huberman, B. (2010). Predicting the future with social media Retrieved from http://arxiv.org/abs/1003.5699/.

Blondel, V. D., Guillaume, J,-L., Lambiotte, R., and Lefebvre, E. (2008). Fast unfolding of communities in large networks. *Journal of Statistical Mechanics: Theory and Experiment*, 2008(10), P10008.

Bollen, J., Mao, H., and Zeng, X,-J. (2011). Twitter mood predict the stock market. *Journal of Computational Science*, 2(1), 1–8. Retrieved from doi:10.1016/j .jocs.2010.12.007.

Choi, H., and Varian, H. (2011). (Tech Rep.) *Predicting the Present with Google Trends*. Google Inc.

Da, Z., Engelberand, J., and Gao, P. (2011). In search of attention. *Journal of Finance*, 66(5), 1461–99.

Da, Z., Engelberand, J., and Gao, P. (2015). The sum of all fears: investor sentiment and asset prices. *Review of Financial Studies*, 28(1), 1–32.

Daas, P., and Puts, M. (2014). Social media sentiment and consumer confidence. *European Central Bank Workshop on Using Big Data for Forecasting and Statistics*, 5, 1–26.

Das, S. R., and Chen, M. Y. (2007). Yahoo! for Amazon: sentiment extraction from small talk on the web. *Management Science*, 53(9), 1375–88.

Eagle, N., Macy, M., and Claxton, R. (2010). Network diversity and economic development. *Science*, 328, 1029–31.

Ettredge, M., Gerdes, J., and Karuga, G. (2005). Using web-based search data to prediction macroeconomic statistics. *Communication of the ACM*, 48(11), 87–92.

Gilbert, E., and Karahalios, K. (2010). Widespread worry and the stock market. *Proceedings of the International Conference on Weblogs and Social Media*, 2(1), 229–47.

Graesser, J., Cheriyadat, A., Vatsavai, R. R., Chandola, V., Long, J., and Bright, E. (2012). Image based characterization of formal and informal neighborhoods in an urban landscape. *IEEE Journal of Selected Topics in Applied Earth Observations and Remote Sensing*, 5(4), 1164–76.

Gruhl, D., Guha, R., Kumar, R., Novak, J., and Tomkins, A. (2005). The predictive power of online chatter. In *KDD '05: Proceedings of the Eleventh ACM SIGKDD International Conference on Knowledge Discovery in Data Mining* (pp. 78–87). ACM. Retrieved from http://dx.doi.org/10.1145/1081870.1081883 doi 10.1145/1081870.1081883.

Karabulut, Y. (2011). *Can Facebook Predict Stock Market Activity?* SSRN eLibrary.

Lazer, D., Kennedy, R., King, G., and Vespignani, A. (2014). The parable of Google flu: traps in big data analysis. *Science*, 343 (6176), 1203–5. Retrieved from http://www.sciencemag.org/content/343/6176/1203.short APACrefDOI 10.1126/ science.1248506.

Lazer, D., Pentland, A., Adamic, L., Aral, S., Barabási, A. L., Brewer, D., and Van Alstyne, M. (2009). Computational social science. *Science*, 323(5915), 721–3.

Long, B., Shleifer, A., Summers, L., and Waldmann, R. (1990). Noise trader risk in financial markets. *Journal of Political Economy*, 98(4), 703–38.

Mao, H., Counts, S., and Bollen, J. (2014). Quantifying the effects of online bullishness on international financial markets. *European Central Bank Workshop on Using Big Data for Forecasting and Statistics*. Retrieved from https://www.ecb.europa.eu/events/pdf/conferences/140407/Mao_Quantifying TheEffectsOfOnlineBullishnessOnInternationalFinancialMarkets.pdf?83253ef75 e1a6349c3cfa4cc76addad.

Mao, Y., Wei, W., Wang, B., and Liu, B. (2012) Correlating S&P 500 stocks with Twitter data. In *Proceedings of the First ACM International Workshop on Hot Topics on Interdisciplinary Social Networks* (pp. 69–72). ACM.

Newman, M. E. J. (2003). The structure and function of complex networks: the structure and function of complex networks. *SIAM Review*, 45(2), 167–256.

O'Connor, B., Balasubramanyan, R., Routledge, B. R., & Smith, N. A. (2010). From tweets to polls: linking text sentiment to public opinion time series. In *Proceedings of the International Conference on Weblogs and Social Media* (pp. 122–9). AAAI Press.

Oh, C., and Sheng, O. R. L. (2011). Investigating predictive power of stock micro blog sentiment in forecasting future stock price directional movement. *ICIS 2011 Proceedings* (pp. 57–8). ICIS.

Page, S. (2007). *The Difference: How the Power of Diversity Creates Better Groups, Firms, Schools and Societies*. Princeton University Press.

Pang, B., and Lee, L. (2008). Opinion mining and sentiment analysis. *Foundations and Trends in Information Retrieval*, 2(1–2), 1–135.

Preis, T., Moat, H. S., Stanley, H. E., and Bishop, S. R. (2012). Quantifying the advantage of looking forward. *Scientific Reports*, 2, 350.

Ruiz, E. J., Hristidis, V., Castillo, C., Gionis, A., and Jaimes, A. (2012). Correlating financial time series with micro-blogging activity. In *Proceedings of the Fifth ACM International Conference on Web Search and Data Mining* (pp. 513–22). ACM.

Sul, H., Dennis, A. R., and Yuan, L. I. (2014). Trading on Twitter: the financial information content of emotion in social media. In *47th Hawaii International Conference on System Sciences (HICSS), 2014* (pp. 806–15). IEEE.

Vatsavai, R. R. (2013). Gaussian multiple instance learning approach for mapping the slums of the world using very high resolution imagery. In *Proceedings of the 19th ACM SIGKDD International Conference on Knowledge Discovery and Data Mining* (pp. 1419–26). ACM.

Zhang, X., Fuehres, H., and Gloor, P. (2010). Predicting stock market indicators through Twitter: "I hope it is not as bad as I fear." *Social and Behavioral Sciences*, 26, 55–62.

4

Hyperlocal Happiness from Tweets

Daniele Quercia

It has been hypothesized that the language of Twitter users is associated with the socioeconomic well-being those users experience in their physical communities (e.g., satisfaction with life in their states of residence). To test the relationship between language use and psychological experience, researchers textually processed tweets to extract mainly sentiment and subject matters (topics) and associated those two quantities with census indicators of well-being. They did so by focusing on geographically coarse-grained communities, the finest-grained of which were U.S. census areas. After briefly introducing those studies and describing the common steps they generally take, we offer a case study taken from our own work on geographically smaller communities: London census areas.

1. Introduction

Happiness has often been indirectly characterized by readily quantifiable economic indicators such as gross domestic product (GDP). Yet in recent years, policy makers have tried to change that and introduced indicators that go beyond merely economic considerations. In 2010, the former French president Nicolas Sarkozy intended to include well-being in France's measurement of economic progress (Stratton, 2010). The UK prime minister David Cameron has been initiating a series of policies, under the rubric "Big Society," that seek to make society stronger by getting more people running their own affairs locally all together. The idea shared by many governments all over the world is to explore new ways of measuring community well-being and, as such, put forward policies that promote more quality of life (happiness) rather than material welfare (GDP).

Measuring the well-being of single individuals can be successfully accomplished by administering questionnaires such as the Satisfaction with Life (SWL) test, whose score effectively reflects the extent to which a person feels that his or her life is worthwhile (Diener, Diener, & Diener, 1995). To go beyond single individuals and measure the well-being of communities, one could administer SWL tests to community residents. But that would be costly and is thus done on limited population samples and once per year at best.

Researchers have recently shown that the cost problem can be ameliorated by monitoring implicit data generated by community members on social media. For the social sciences, social media sites host a collective, open recording of an enormous number of digital interactions, making it possible to quantitatively characterize previously unobservable microscale communication mechanisms (Pentland, 2014).

This chapter introduces the use of text analysis to track happiness of Twitter users. Given the difficulty of georeferencing tweets, most of the previous work has focused on coarse-grained geographic units, typically entire countries. Schwartz et al. (2013) took a step further by considering U.S. counties and relating their use of language on Twitter to their collective well-being. In so doing, they found many patterns that had been previously observed in the well-being literature: words related to prosocial activities, exercise, and, more generally, engagement with life predicted higher life satisfaction, while words of disengagement in a county predicted lower life satisfaction.

After presenting the main insights of previous studies, this chapter unfolds in a way similar to what a typical study in this research area would. That is, we start by introducing how to crawl, clean, and map tweets and then how to model the use of language in them. Departing from the literature's typical focus on coarse-grained geographic communities, we offer a case study that entails a finer-grained geographic level, that of UK census areas (as a reference, consider that a London neighborhood is generally divided in multiple census areas). We highlight the main insights learned from this case study and conclude by discussing the main shortcomings that might well drive future work.

2. Twitter Happiness

There has been considerable work related to the subject matter of this chapter. Dodds et al. (2011) analyzed text on tweets to remotely sense societal-scale levels of happiness and study how word use changed as a function of time. They collected tweets posted over a thirty-three month span (from September 9, 2008, to September 18, 2011) by over 63 million unique users and built a tunable hedonometer that analyzed word usage in real time for assigning happiness scores. They found fascinating temporal variations in happiness over timescales ranging from hours to years. At the year level, they found that, after an upward trend starting from January to April 2009, average happiness gradually decreased. On the other hand, at the month level, they saw average happiness gradually increase over the last months of each year. Finally, at the week level, they found peaks over the weekend and the nadirs on Mondays and Tuesdays. By looking at the day level, they were able to show that negative days were seen during unexpected societal trauma such as the 2008 bailout of the U.S. financial system, the 2009 swine flu or H1N1 pandemic, the February 2010 Chilean earthquake, the October 2010 storm across the United States, the March 2011 earthquake and tsunami in Japan, and the 2011 killing of Osama Bin Laden.

Lansdall-Welfare Lampos, and Cristianini (2012) analyzed 484 million tweets generated by more than 9.8 million users from the United Kingdom over thirty-one months to study the impact of the economic downturn and social tensions on the use of language. More specifically, they studied the use of emotion words classified in four categories taken from the tool WordNet Affect: anger, fear, joy, and sadness. The results were 146 anger words, 92 fear words, 224 joy words, and 115 sadness words. The authors found that periodic events such as Christmas, Valentine's Day, and Halloween were associated with very similar use of words, year after year. On the other hand, they observed two main negative change points: one occurring in October 2010, when the government announced cuts to public spending; and the other in summer 2011, when riots broke out in various UK cities. Interestingly, the increased use of negative emotion words preceded, not followed, those events.

Golder and Macy (2011) studied the 500 million English tweets that 2.4 million users produced during almost two years. Based on their hour-by-hour analysis, they found that offline patterns of mood variations also hold on Twitter: mood variations were associated with seasonal changes in day length. People also changed their mood as the working day progressed and were happier during weekends.

Schwartz et al. (2013) tested whether the language used in tweets is predictive of the subjective well-being of people living in U.S. counties. They did so by collecting a random sample of tweets in 1,293 U.S. counties between November 2008 and January 2010. By correlating the word use with subjective well-being as measured by representative surveys, they found positive correlations with prosocial activities, exercise, and engagement with personal and work life and negative correlations with words of disengagement. Those findings were in line with existing well-being studies in the social sciences.

Frank et al. (2013) characterized the mobility patterns of 180,000 individuals. In so doing, the researchers were able to characterize changes in the use of language as a function of movement. They found that tweets written close to a user's center of mass (typical location) are slightly happier than those written 1 kilometer away, which is the distance representative of a short daily commute to work. Beyond identifying this least-happy distance, they found that the use of positive emotion words increased logarithmically with distance. This pattern continued to hold when they studied a user's radius of movement. The larger a user's radius, the happier the words the user tended to use.

Finally, De Choudhury Monroy-Hernández, and Mark (2014) studied whether people exposed to chronic violence lowered affective responses in their Twitter posts. To this end, they collected all of the Spanish tweets that were mentioning one of the four Mexican cities of Monterrey, Reynosa, Saltillo, and Veracruz. Between August 2010 and December 2012, these four cities were affected by protracted violence in the context of the "Mexican Drug War." The researchers found that, while violence was on the rise offline, negative emotional expression online was declining and emotional arousal and dominance were rising: both aspects are known psychological correlates of population desensitization. This suggests that chronic exposure to violence is indeed associated with signs of desensitization in social media postings.

Having briefly reviewed part of the well-being studies on Twitter, we are now ready to introduce the three main preliminary steps those studies generally take: crawling, cleaning, and mapping tweets.

3. Crawling, Cleaning, and Mapping

3.1. *Crawling*

To analyze tweets, one needs to collect them to start with. A typical way of crawling (collecting) Twitter data is to use its public API (as Chapter 1 details). Researchers often do so by selecting seed profiles (e.g., accounts followed by many users, such as those of news outlets) and crawling all the users who follow those seed profiles. Since the API is rate-limited, only a restricted number of tweets can be collected. To partly fix that, in February 2014, Twitter announced that it will make all its tweets, dating back to 2006, freely available to researchers (Moyer, 2014).

3.2. *Cleaning*

After collecting tweets, one needs to clean them. This is often done in two main steps. First, profiles that are likely to be spam accounts or are not of real people are filtered away. One way of doing so is to filter away profiles with very low numbers of followers (compared to their following counts). An alternative way is to use third-party services. For example, PeerIndex is able to associate a "realness score" to a Twitter profile. This score is generated upon information such as whether the profile has been self-certified on the PeerIndex site and or has been linked to Facebook or LinkedIn. "PeerIndex realness score is a metric that indicates the likelihood that the profile is of a real person, rather than a spambot or Twitter feed. A score above 50 means this account is of a real person, a score below 50 means it is less likely to be a real person."[1]

The second cleaning step deals with the text in the tweets. This step is generally carried out by preprocessing the corpus of tweets with a standard pipeline. More specifically, the text is converted to lowercase and tokenized around both whitespace and common punctuation. Any token with a leading @ character is discarded, as this is simply the username of another Twitter user. Each token is then stripped of its remaining punctuation and compared to a list of common English stopwords (specifically, those used by MySQL 5.65[2]), as well as a list of Twitter-specific stopwords (such as "rt," which is a common token signifying that the tweet containing it is a retweet and has been forwarded from another Twitter user). All nonstopword tokens are retained.

3.3. *Georeferencing*

After being collected and cleaned, tweets need to be mapped within the bounding box of the geographic unit of analysis. If the unit is country or city, then the free text entry of a home city on a profile is often used. At finer geographic resolutions (e.g., counties, census areas, neighborhoods), one should resort to the tweets that have geolocation coordinates as well; those tweets represent only a small fraction of the overall tweets, however.

One very important yet often overlooked aspect is that georeferencing tweets (as opposed to profiles) results in a sample of users who happen to be in, for example, a neighborhood rather than of users who live in it. This difference becomes crucial whenever the distinction between residents and visitors impacts the results of the analysis. Past work has shown that topical words mentioned on Twitter by residents and by visitors are quite different, and that can be visually seen by comparing the following picture pairs: Figure 4.1a versus Figure 4.1c related to well-to-do areas, and Figure 4.1b versus Figure 4.1d related to deprived areas (Quercia, Séeaghda, & Crowcroft, 2012). In

---

[1]   http://www.peerindex.net/help/scores.
[2]   http://dev.mysql.com/doc/refman/5.6/en/fulltext-stopwords.html.

Figure 4.1. Tag clouds of topical words *mentioned* by *residents* and visitors of deprived and well-to-do London communities.
Word size is proportional to the correlation with deprivation/well-being scores.

Figure 4.1d, we see the topical marker "c2c," which is generated by youngsters going from their well-to-do residential area in Essex to central London on the c2c train line which goes through several deprived areas in London. They are visitors of those deprived communities, and what they talk about differs from what residents of those communities talk about. Yet, the methodology often found in the literature mixes those visitors' tweets with residents'.

4. Modeling the Use of Language

4.1. *Use of Language*

Researchers in social psychology have found a link between well-being of individuals and their use of words. To a certain extent, "our words reflect ourselves," to paraphrase the title of Henrich, Heine, and Norenzayan's 2003 work. The number of first-person pronouns (e.g., "I," "my") in speech or writing often correlates with narcissism and with the personality trait of "Neuroticism" (Weintraub, 1989; Stirman & Pennebaker, 2001). Second-person pronouns (e.g., "you") and third-person pronouns (e.g., "she," "they") are markers of social engagement and have been found to correlate negatively with depression (Rude, Gortner, & Pennebaker, 2004). Furthermore, words that express positive emotions (e.g., "good," "happy") are used more by people who are satisfied with their lives (Pennebaker and King, 1999).

To quantify the use of those textual markers, over decades, social psychologists populated a dictionary called "Linguistic Inquiry Word Count" (LIWC).[3] LIWC is a standard dictionary of 2,300 English words that capture 80 percent of the words used in everyday conversations and reflect people's emotional and cognitive perceptions. These words fall into seventy-two categories, such as positive and negative emotional words and words about work, school, and money. Note that, rather than grouping words based on their material subject matter (e.g., "sports," "technology"), LIWC categories are generally abstract and based on linguistic and psychological processes. For example, there exist categories for cognitive processes (such as "insight" and "certainty"), psychological constructs (e.g., "affect," "cognition"), as well as personal concerns (e.g., "work," "home," "leisure activities"). Each word may thus belong to multiple categories; for example, the prefix entry "hostil*" belongs to the categories "affect" (affective processes), "negemo" (negative emotions), and "anger."

Since tweets are short, the finest textual unit of analysis is that of a Twitter profile. Thus, for the tweets in each profile, one typically counts the number of words matching the LIWC categories and computes the normalized fraction of each category's count (i.e., *z-score* for category *c*), as shown in Equation 4.1.

$$f_c = \frac{w_c - \mu_c}{\sigma_c} \tag{4.1}$$

where w_c is the fraction of words classified in category c (over the total number of classified words) for the profile; μ_c is the fraction of words in category c, averaged across all profiles; and σ_c is the corresponding standard deviation.

4.2. Sentiment

The most widely used LIWC categories are those related to emotion words. That is because they are used to build simple sentiment classifiers purely based on word count. For each profile, the number of words that are positive and those that are negative (words matching the two categories of "positive emotions" and "negative emotions" as defined in LIWC) are counted, and those two counts are then aggregated to produce the profile's sentiment score (Kramer, 2010). This score is $(f_p - f_n)$, where f_p is the z-score for the category "positive emotions" and f_p is the z-score for "negative emotions." The z-score normalization

---

[3]   www.liwc.net.

using means and standard deviations accounts for the unbalanced distribution of positive and negative words of the English language (Kramer, 2010).

A limitation of word count is that the vocabulary it uses (in this case, LIWC) does not contain all English words that are positive or negative. To expand that vocabulary, Dodds et al. (2011) have recently used the crowdsourcing platform of Amazon's Mechanical Turk[4] and obtained happiness ratings for 10,222 individual words. They did so by asking users on Mechanical Turk to rate how a given word made them feel on a nine-point integer scale, obtaining fifty independent evaluations per word. In the supplementary information of their article (Dodds et al., 2011), they provided happiness averages and standard deviations for all the words.

Also see Section 4.2 in Chapter 1 on the topic of sentiment analysis for further discussion on this topic.

4.3. *Topic Modeling*

To go beyond sentiment and extract the *subject matter* of tweets, researchers have often used topic models (Ramage, Dumais, & Liebling, 2010). Latent Dirichlet Allocation (LDA) is the most commonly used unsupervised generative topic model (Blei, Ng, & Jordan, 2003). It is capable of learning the implicit categories present within discrete datasets (such as corpora of Twitter profiles). It assumes that each profile consists of a mixture of corpus-wide topics, and that each instance of a word in a profile pertains to exactly one of these topics. Given a corpus of profiles, LDA can infer the underlying distribution of topics in each profile, as well as the distribution of words in each topic.

The topics of an LDA model are probability distributions over a vocabulary. Words that tend to co-occur will have high associated probabilities in the topics to which they pertain – for example, "Facebook" and "Twitter" will often co-occur, just as each will often co-occur with the word "social." Neither, however, would be expected to appear often alongside, for example, "econometrics" – the first three terms are part of a different topic to the fourth. There may therefore exist a topic representing the social elements in the corpus that assigns high probabilities to the former words and low probability to the latter. The way in which LDA clusters terms into topics depends on its parameters, particularly the number of topics. This is typically set to 50, 100, or 200. If we build a model with only a few topics, each will embody a separate category on a broad scale, whereas models with more topics are capable of learning subcategories and more subtle relationships between words.

---

[4] www.mturk.com.

At times, however, LDA alone cannot easily assign topics to Twitter profiles. The topics it learns are unlabeled; without labels, the inferred subject matter of a profile cannot be succinctly described. Consequently, several modifications of LDA to incorporate supervision have been proposed. Ramage Dumais, and Liebling (2010) put forward L-LDA and applied it to the tasks of finding and following new users and topics and of filtering feeds. This model has been shown to work quite well on tweets since, as opposed to a support vector machine (SVM), it effectively deals with short pieces of text when the training set at hand is limited (Quercia, Askham, & Crowcroft, 2012).

After those initial steps, the sentiment scores or topic distributions for individual Twitter profiles are then aggregated at the geographic unit of analysis. The resulting aggregations are finally correlated with well-being indicators from the census. In interpreting the results, one should consider that correlations between use of language and psychologically based variables (e.g., individual satisfaction with life, community well-being) rarely exceed an r of 0.4 (Meyer et al., 2001).

5. Case Study: Hyperlocal Happiness

Next, we will present a case study whose goal is to focus on small geographic units of analysis. We do so by dwelling on our own work on the relationship between use of language in Twitter and socioeconomic deprivation of London neighborhoods.

5.1. *Main Findings*

We used the Indices of Multiple Deprivation (IMD) as a well-being measure of census communities. Since 2000, the UK Office for National Statistics has published, every three or four years, IMD, a set of indicators that measure deprivation of small census areas in England known as Lower-layer Super Output Areas (Mclennan et al., 2011). These census areas were designed to have a roughly uniform population distribution so that a fine-grained comparison of the relative deprivation of different parts of England is possible. The formulation of the IMD follows the principles set out by Townsend (1987), in which the author argues that deprivation ought to be defined in such a way that it captures the effects of several different factors. In particular, the IMD consists of the following seven components, here listed with examples (not exhaustive) of factors they measure:

Income Deprivation – the number of people claiming income support, child
   tax credits, or asylum;

Employment Deprivation – the number of claimants of a jobseeker's allow-
   ance or incapacity benefit;

Health Deprivation and Disability – a standard measure of premature death,
   the rate of adults suffering mood and anxiety disorders;

Education, Skills, and Training Deprivation – education level attainment,
   the proportion of working adults with no qualifications;

Barriers to Housing and Services – homelessness, overcrowding, distance
   to essential services;

Crime – rates of different kinds of criminal act;

Living Environment Deprivation – housing condition, air quality, rate of
   road traffic accidents.

Finally, there is a composite measure that is a weighted mean of those seven
domains.

Our work considered a census area to be a community. We chose such a
definition of community because it has been widely used in studies of social
deprivation (for example, by Eagle, Macy, & Claxton, 2010), and because
using IMD scores with any other definition of community would lead to results
that are not ecologically valid. To georeference profiles at the level of neighborhood, our work considered the free text "home location" entries on profiles
and converted textual strings containing city names and neighborhood names
into longitude/latitude pairs with the Yahoo! PlaceMaker API.[5]

Upon our correlation analysis, we found that the higher the normalized
sentiment score of a community's tweets, the higher the community's socioeconomic well-being. The correlation coefficients were statistically significant
and were as high as $r = 0.350$. These results suggested that monitoring the
sentiment of tweets may well be an accurate and cost-effective way of tracking the well-being of communities. They ultimately suggested that users in
more deprived London communities tweet, on average, more negatively than
those in less-deprived communities. Also, there was no correlation between
one area's number of Twitter profiles and its IMD. By contrast, the mobile
phone brand made the difference: in deprived communities, Blackberry phones
were widely used, while in well-to-do ones, iPhone usage was predominant.

To go beyond sentiment, we also studied the relationship between topics
(extracted by LDA) and socioeconomic well-being. We found that certain topics were correlated (positively and negatively) with community deprivation.

---

[5] geo.placemaker functionality under http://developer.yahoo.com/yql/console/.

Users in more deprived community tweeted about wedding parties, matters expressed in Spanish or Portuguese, and celebrity gossips. By contrast, those in less-deprived communities tweeted about vacations, professional use of social media, environmental issues, sports, and health issues (Quercia, Séeaghda, & Crowcroft, 2012).

That last set of results was obtained by georeferencing Twitter profiles. We did so to focus our study on community residents. To then consider visitors and study whether those visiting deprived areas (people who happen to be in such areas) and those visiting less-deprived areas talk about different things, we considered the topics expressed in georeferenced tweets (not profiles). By correlating topic distributions and IMD, we found previously unobserved topics that were likely to be associated with visitors rather than residents: one such topic reflected slang expressions used by travelers on the *c2c* train line, which goes from Fenchurch Street railway station through (socially deprived) East London to the (well-to-do) Essex area.

We finally showed that monitoring the subject matter of tweets not only offers insights into community well-being, but also is a reasonable way of predicting community deprivation scores. To that end, we built a regression model that predicted IMD as a linear combination of the normalized fractions of all topics. The extent to which the regression predicts IMD was reflected in a measure called R^2 – the higher R^2, the better the fit of the model. In our case, $R^2 = .32$ for residents' tweets, suggesting that the topics discussed by a community's residents explained a considerable share or variance of the community's IMD (roughly 32 percent of it). Using fewer topics as predictors – such as the eleven most correlated topics – still resulted into R^2 being as high as .30, suggesting that the predictive ability did not significantly depend on the number of predictors used.

5.2. Implications

Our results suggest that it is possible to track the emotional health of local communities effectively from their residents' tweets in an unobtrusive way, as tweets are publicly available and easy to crawl.

The significance of the results extends beyond merely tracking emotional health of local areas: they provide evidence that users' offline communities have a noticeable effect on their online interactions. To appreciate the importance of this insight, consider that past research has focused on studying two relevant relationships. The first is between where people live and their subjective well-being: income inequality, unemployment rates, urbanization, safety, and deprivation of an area have all been shown to relate to people's subjective well-being across different countries and time periods (Dolan, Peasgood, & White, 2008). The second relationships is between subjective well-being and what people write on social media: sentiment expressed in user-generated content gets more positive as people are increasingly satisfied with their lives (Kramer, 2010). From these two relationships, a third one might transitively follow but has never been tested: the relationships between where people live and the social media content they generate. We have now tested this third relation and found that, indeed, tweets from residents of socially deprived communities contain more negative emotions than those from residents of well-off communities.

6. Discussion

While evidence suggests that an online platform such as Twitter has observable connections with the objective physical reality of a neighborhood, analysts (let alone policy makers) will have to remain cognizant of three main shortcomings.

6.1. *Causality*

Our results do not speak of causality. Though the causal direction is difficult to be determined from observational data, one could repeatedly crawl Twitter over multiple time intervals and use a cross-lag analysis to observe potential causal relationships. Causal claims are not only essential for policy making, but also desirable for building effective tracking applications. The algorithms behind Google Flu trends are still being tweaked as they occasionally over- or underestimate flu rates due to popular media sources influencing search patterns (Butler, 2013). Such a tweaking is necessary because those algorithms are not meant to disentangle causes and correlations – they are simply based on observed correlations. Models strictly based on causal claims are more likely to be robust against prediction noise as they are based on the root causes of the phenomenon under study.

6.2. *Sample Representativeness*

Twitter users represent a nonrepresentative subpopulation of all people: 63 percent of Twitter users are less than thirty-five years old and 58 percent have a total household income of at least $60,000 in the United States.[6] By contrast, in 2012, the median household income was roughly $51,000 and the median

---

[6] http://blog.site-seeker.com/who-uses-twitter-demographic/.

age was 36.8 years.[7] Our results thus disproportionately reflect the "happiness" of some citizens over others. To partly tackle this issue, future studies need to meet two main criteria. First, they need to be carried out in geographic areas that have considerable Twitter penetration rates (e.g., we chose London because it was the top Twitter-using city in the world at the beginning of 2010; Butcher, 2009). Second, they should be thoroughly tested for external validity: that is, their results should be consistent with well-being findings from other methodologies.

6.3. Beyond USA or UK

So far, researchers have studied users in UK and United States. Cities in emerging markets, most of which are in developing countries, have been overlooked. These cities are of increasing interest since they will account for nearly 40 percent of the global growth in the next fifteen years (Dobbs, Remes, & Smit, 2011): the Boston Consulting Group has classified as many as thirty-four Brazilian cities as emerging markets (Jin et al., 2011). That is why we have recently focused on Brazil (Vaca, 2014), a fast-growing developing country that has become the second-biggest market, outside United States, for social media sites such as Twitter.[8]

7. Conclusion

Our digital footprints have been used to tackle fundamental research questions. Studying the relationship between offline community well-being and online use of language is a case in point. However, the willingness to adopt digital footprints for research should go hand in hand with new methodological contributions. A few methodological questions that need to be answered include:

> Which are the main obstacles to the accurate estimation of causal effects? By analyzing the human experience from online data, researchers are able to identify patterns, but working out relationships is more difficult, and causality is hard to establish. In the last decades, there has been a considerable refinement in the statistical tools for inferring causality in observational datasets. In particular, the use of instrumental variables has

---

[7] http://en.wikipedia.org/wiki/Household_income_in_the_United_States.
[8] http://thenextweb.com/twitter/2013/01/16/twitter-to-open-office-in-brazil-its-second-biggest-market-after-the-us-in-accounts/.

become popular among economists. Under which conditions are such tools effective? By contrast, when are web-based experiments with controlled assignment of treatments to subjects the only way to go?

How do we increase the pool of subjects being studied? Social media research has mainly focused on users in countries that have high penetration rates of social media sites (e.g., the UK, the United States, South Korea). How about the remaining countries, especially the developing ones?

How do we generalize the observations learned from online studies to the offline world?

The opportunities and challenges of studying people's digital footprints are extraordinary – enough to make any researcher happy.

References

Blei, D. M., Ng, A. Y., and Jordan, M. I. (2003). Latent Dirichlet Allocation. *Journal Machine Learning Research*, 3, 993–1022.

Butcher, M. (2009). London is the capital of Twitter, says founder. *TechCrunch Europe*.

Butler, D. (2013). When Google got flu wrong. *Nature*, 494, 155–6.

De Choudhury, M., Monroy-Hernández, A., and Mark, G. (2014). "Narco" emotions: affect and desensitization in social media during the Mexican Drug War. In *Proceedings of the ACM SIGCHI Conference on Human Factors in Computing Systems (CHI)* (pp. 3563–72). ACM.

Diener, E., Diener, M., and Diener, C. (1995). Factors predicting the subjective well-being of nations. *Journal of Personality and Social Psychology*, 69(5), 851–64.

Dobbs, R., Remes, J., and Smit, S. (2011). The world's new growth frontier: midsize cities in emerging markets. *McKinsey Quarterly*, http://www.mckinsey.com.

Dodds, P. S., Harris, K. D., Kloumann, I. M., Bliss, C. A., and Danforth, C. M. (2011). Temporal patterns of happiness and information in a global social network: hedonometrics and Twitter. *PLOS ONE*, 6(12), e26752.

Dolan, P., Peasgood, T., and White, M. (2008). Do we really know what makes us happy? A review of the economic literature on the factors associated with subjective well-being. *Journal of Economic Psychology*, 29(1), 94–122.

Eagle, N., Macy, M., and Claxton, R. (2010). Network diversity and economic development. *Science*, 328(5981), 1029–31.

Frank, M. R., Mitchell, L., Dodds, P. S., and Danforth, C. M. (2013). Happiness and the patterns of life: a study of geolocated tweets. *Scientific Reports*, 3(2625), doi:10.1038/srep02625.

Golder, S. A. and Macy, M. W. (2011). Diurnal and seasonal mood vary with work, sleep, and daylength across diverse cultures. *Science*, 333(6051), 1878–81.

Henrich, J., Heine, S., and Norenzayan, A. (2003). Psychological aspects of natural language use: our words, our selves. *Annual Review Psychology*, 54, 547–77.

Jin, D., Michael, D., Foo, P., Guevara, J., Peña, I., Tratz, A., and Verma, S. (2011). Winning in emerging-market cities: a guide to the world's largest growth opportunity. http://www.bcg.com. Boston Consulting Group.

Kramer, A. (2010). An unobtrusive behavioral model of "Gross National Happiness." In *Proceedings of the 28th ACM CHI.* (pp. 287–90). ACM.

Lansdall-Welfare, T. O., Lampos, V., and Cristianini, N. (2012). Effects of the recession on public mood in the UK. *Social Media Applications in News and Entertainment (SMANE) at ACM WWW.*

Mclennan, D., Barnes, H., Noble, M., Davies, J., and Garratt, E. (2011). *The English Indices of Deprivation 2010.* UK Office for National Statistics.

Meyer, G. J., Finn, S. E., Eyde, L. D., Kay, G. G., Moreland, K. L., Dies, R. R., Eisman, E. J., Kubiszyn, T. W., and Reed, G. M. (2001). Psychological testing and psychological assessment: a review of evidence and issues. *American Psychologist,* 56(2), 128–65.

Moyer, M. W. (2014). Twitter to release all tweets to scientists. *Scientific American,* 310(6).

Pennebaker, J. and King, L. (1999). Linguistic styles: language use as an individual difference. *Journal of Personality and Social Psychology,* 77(6), 1296–312.

Pentland, A. (2014). *Social Physics: How Ideas Turn into Action.* Penguin.

Quercia, D., Askham, H., and Crowcroft, J. (2012). TweetLDA: supervised topic classification and link prediction in Twitter. In *Proceedings of the 4th Annual ACM Web Science Conference (WebSci)* (pp. 247–50). ACM.

Quercia, D., Séeaghda, D. O., and Crowcroft, J. (2012). Talk of the city: our tweets, our community happiness. In *Proceedings of the 6th International AAAI Conference on Weblogs and Social Media.* AAAI.

Ramage, D., Dumais, S., and Liebling, D. (2010). Characterizing microblogs with topic models. In *Proceedings of the Fourth International AAAI Conference on Weblogs and Social Media.* AAAI.

Rude, S., Gortner, E., and Pennebaker, J. (2004). Language use of depressed and depression-vulnerable college students. *Cognition and Emotion,* 18(8), 1121–33.

Schwartz, H. A., Eichstaedt, J. C., Kern, M. L., Dziurzynski, L., Lucas, R. E., Agrawal, M., Park, G. J., Lakshmikanth, S. K., Jha, S., Seligman, M. E. P., and Ungar, L. H. (2013). Characterizing geographic variation in well-being using tweets. In *Proceedings of the Seventh International AAAI Conference on Weblogs and Social Media.* AAAI.

Stirman, S., and Pennebaker, J. (2001). Word use in the poetry of suicidal and nonsuicidal poets. *Psychosomatic Medicine,* 63, 517–22.

Stratton, A. (2010). Happiness index to gauge Britain's national mood. *Guardian,* November 2010.

Townsend, P. (1987). Deprivation. *Journal of Social Policy,* 16, 125–46.

Vaca, C., Quercia, D., Aiello, L. M., and Fraternali, P. (2014). Taking Brazils pulse: tracking growing urban economies from online attention. In *Proceedings of the 23rd ACM Conference on World Wide Web (WWW) Companion* (pp. 451–6). ACM.

Weintraub, W. (1989). *Verbal Behavior in Everyday Life.* Springer.

5

Public Health

Patty Kostkova

Twitter, crowdsourcing, and other medical technology inventions producing real-time geolocated streams of personalized data have changed the way we think about health (Kostkova 2015). However, Twitter's strength is its two-way communication nature – both as a health information source but also as a central hub for the creation and dissemination of media health coverage. Health authorities, insurance companies, marketing agencies, and individuals can leverage the availability of large datasets from Twitter to improve early warning services and preparedness, aid disease prevalence mapping, and provide personal targeted health advice, as well as influence public sentiment about major health interventions. However, despite the growing potential, there are still many challenges to address to develop robust and reliable systems integrating Twitter streams to real-world provision of healthcare.

1. Introduction

Health and well-being are top priorities for citizens, societies, and governments from individual to national and international levels. In particular, public health threats have become a focus due to globalization, the emergence of new diseases, and the reappearance of older infectious diseases. The SARS outbreak in 2003 illustrated how quickly a new virus could spread globally.

The growth of the Internet and social networks has enabled unprecedented support for individual health monitoring and personalized care, as well as large-scale public health measures (Smith & Christakis, 2008; Valente, 2010; Paul & Dredze, 2011). In particular, the role of Twitter in the health domain now encompasses a two-way channel for managing health and seeking health advice at the personal level on one hand, and for aiding early warning and out-break response systems with the aim of mobilizing knowledge and scientific expertise to protect populations on the other hand.

The spectrum of Twitter health research outreach is impressive. Paul and Drezde (2011) investigated how Twitter became an important medium for understanding concerns about public health, while Christakis and Fawler (2007, 2008) looked into the dynamics of health behavior on a large social network investigating smoking and obesity. De Quincey et al. (2014) and Takahashi, Abe, and Igata (2011) investigated the potential of Twitter to map hay fever, and Sadilek and Kautz (2013) demonstrated the impact of external factors such as pollution and the use of public transport on health.

However, the major focus of Twitter use in the real-world healthcare system has been centered on three topics.

Firstly, social networks have attracted a great deal of interest as a possible source of data for epidemic intelligence (EI), demonstrating it can enhance early warning outbreak detection systems through real-time large-scale popu-lation monitoring in order to predict the spread of the diseases.

The second challenge is using Twitter as a health news dissemination chan-nel, in particular for health risk communication. Governments no longer have complete control over what is published by the media and how it is accessed. Twitter allows global populations to create and share content without editorial comment or moderation, which is of key importance during emergencies and public health dangers. However, this raises concerns over the quality of infor-mation shared via Twitter.

This leads us to the third opportunity – measuring sentiment on major health concerns such as vaccination. Users now have the difficult task of assessing the quality of the information they see without any specific medical training. They are often subject to false information, scare-mongering, and false adver-tising. A recent example is the widespread support that can be found online that ignores scientific evidence and claims that there is a link between measles, mumps, and rubella (MMR) vaccine and autism. The impact of this can be seen in the UK by the increased cases of mumps and whooping cough and the return of previously eradicated infectious diseases, such as measles. However, understanding the communities' influence and sentiment can direct local pub-lic health communication and control measures where most needed.

This chapter is organized as follows. The next section discusses the role of Twitter as an early warning system through a case study from the 2009 swine flu pandemic. We next discuss the role of Twitter in the dissemination of infor-mation of public health importance with a case study highlighting the role of Twitter for disseminating the World Health Organization (WHO) declaration of swine flu as a global pandemics on June 11, 2009. Further, we cover sentiment analysis and vaccination as a case study. The chapter concludes with discussion and future work.

2. Twitter – Early Warning and Preparedness

Epidemic intelligence (EI) is the automated identification of health threats and disease outbreaks, their verification and risk assessment, and investigation to inform health authorities about the required measure to protect the citizens (Kaiser & Coulombier, 2006; Kaiser et al., 2006; Paquet et al., 2006). For over a decade, electronic EI systems using automated news/media scanning tools have complemented traditional surveillance. However, with the increase in the use of social networks (SN) and user-generated web tools called "Web 2.0" (such as Wikipedia, YouTube, Reddit, Twitter, and Facebook), outbreaks are often discovered earlier through EI Web 2.0 tools than through traditional reporting channels. The potential of digital epidemiology analyzing digital data streams for public health purposes brings great potential and new challenges (Salathé et al., 2012) while creating new possibilities for the use of big data (Hay et al., 2013).

The constantly increasing amount of user-generated content on Twitter provides EI systems with a vital source of real-time geolocated context-aware online activity – the SN revolutionized the speed and timeliness of EI. For public health needs, sampling large populations are the core business that makes Twitter an excellent sampling tool.

In terms of epidemic intelligence, Twitter can be used to both track (de Quincey & Kostkova, 2009; Lampos & Cristianini, 2010; Lampos, de Bie, & Cristianini, 2010) and predict (Szomszor, Kostkova, & de Quincey, 2011) the spread of infectious diseases. We will discuss these studies in detail in the next section. Lampos and Cristianini (2012) used the technique of supervised learning for "nowcasting" events by exploring geolocated Twitter signals for influenza-like illness (ILI) rates. Further, a number of approaches adopted during the swine flu outbreak of 2009 were discussed by the *British Medical Journal* (BMJ), where public health agencies' experts highlighted the potential and practical challenges (Malik, 2011; St. Louis & Zorlu, 2012). Also in the United States, ILI were tracked and correlated with Centers for Disease Prevention and Control (CDC) surveillance data by Culotta (2010), and dengue fever was tracked using Twitter in Brazil by Gomide et al. (2011). Culotta's approach used regression and illustrated strong correlation of the two datasets. The role of travel for seasonal transmission of A(H1N1) was also investigated by Balcan et al. (2009) to provide evidence for potential travel restrictions for policy makers. Recently, Salathé et al. (2013) illustrated the role of digital epidemiology and Twitter for understanding the new strain of influenza A (H7N9) and coronavirus (MERS-CoV).

2.1. *Twitter Predicts a Pandemic – a Case Study*

In this section, we present two studies demonstrating the potential of Twitter to provide an early warning signal during the swine flu pandemic in 2009 (Kostkova, Szomszor, & St. Louis, 2014).

Our research using a dataset collected via the Twitter API in the period of May 7 to December 22, 2009 investigated a subset called "self-reported tweets" (users tweeting that they had the disease, whose tweets includes the phrases "have flu," "have the flu," "have swine flu," and "have the swine flu," in present and past tenses). The investigation demonstrated that these tweets provided a signal indicative of the signal created by the officially reported cases, and by cross-correlating the Twitter dataset with official surveillance, we demonstrated that Twitter detected the upcoming spike in the epidemics up to two weeks in the UK and up to three weeks in the United States.

By relying on self-reporting tweets, we make no estimates of the actual number of cases of the disease. However, for early warning systems, the signal *change* rather than the case numbers is important. We cross-correlated the Twitter self-reporting dataset with the official surveillance data from the UK Health Protection Agency (HPA)[1] collected by the Royal College of General Practitioners (RCGP).[2] The HPA provides weekly reports on the RCGP ILI consultation rates for England and Wales, Scotland, and Northern Ireland. For comparison, we normalized the tweets' signal by calculating the percentage of tweets that are self-reporting flu for each day in our investigation period. By applying this normalization process, we eliminated the impact of global trends in Twitter activity (e.g., spam, increased retweeting, and increased posting of links). In Figure 5.1, the two graphs illustrate the HPA RCGP ILI consultation rate for England and Wales (square points, right axis) and the percentage of Twitter activity reporting flu (triangle points, left axis). There is a strong correlation between the two data sources, including a sharp peak in activity on Twitter (week 28, July 6, 2009), which corresponds to the rapid increase in the number of consultations.

---

[1] HPA has been since restructured and renamed to Public Health England (PHE), but at the time of study it was the HPA. www.hpa.org.uk.

[2] http://www.rcgp.org.uk/.

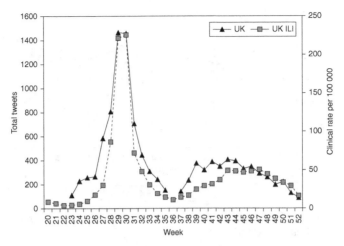

Figure 5.1. A plot showing the RCGP ILI rate for England (square points, right axis) versus self-reported cases on Twitter (triangle points, left axis).

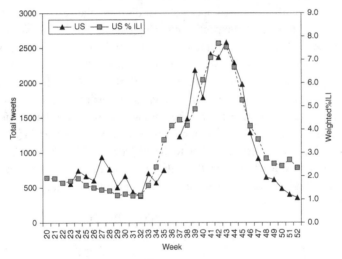

Figure 5.2. A plot showing the ILI rate for the United States (square points, right axis) versus the number of self-reported cases on Twitter (triangle points, left axis).

For the United States, we took self-reporting tweets geolocated within the United States and correlated them with the U.S. surveillance data obtained from the CDC website (http://www.cdc.gov/flu/weekly/), the ILINet (U.S. Outpatient Influenza-like Illness Surveillance Network), as illustrated in Figure 5.2.

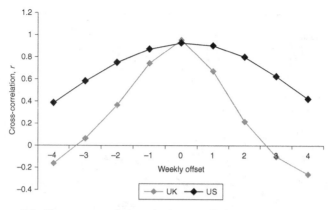

Figure 5.3. The cross-correlation plot between Twitter and the ILI reporting in the UK and the United States.

We quantify the correlation between the two data signals (in our case, Twitter versus official surveillance data) to illustrate the early-warning potential from the "time-lag" perspective by using the normalized cross-correlation formula. We calculated the normalized cross-correlation ratio between various signals from Twitter and the official RCGP UK surveillance data from surveillance and the United States from the CDC ILINet data. Since the data are gathered on a weekly basis, we perform the comparison using a weekly aggregation of Twitter data. Equation 5.1 gives the normalized cross-correlation function r we use, where $x(t)$ is the total number of tweets during week t, and $y(t-i)$ is the number of reported cases according to the HPA or CDC during week $(t-i)$. We calculate r across all flu tweets, those that are self-reporting, those that contain links, and those that are retweets for values of i between -4 and 4.

$$r = \frac{\sum_t (x(t) - \bar{x}) * (y(t-i) - \bar{y})}{\sqrt{\sum_t (x(t) - \bar{x})^2 * \sum_t (y(t-i) - \bar{y})^2}} \qquad (5.1)$$

In Figure 5.3, we display the values of r for weekly offsets between $i = -4$ and $i = 4$. The cross-correlation ratio (or sliding dot product) is a measure of how similar two signals are against a moving time lag. This means that values of r for $i = 0$ represent how much two signals are correlated, when $i = -1$, it represents how much the first signal's last week's value predicts the second signal's current value. Thus, in Figure 5.3 we show that the self-reporting tweets have a strong correlation with the HPA data and CDC data. For early warning systems using social media, we need to focus on the result for negative i, indicating that the Twitter signal predicts the CDC and HPA data by at least one week. There is still a strong correlation at $i = -1$ (when $r = 0.74$) in the UK, indicating that the HPA surveillance data could be predicted by Twitter up to a week in advance. In the United States, the cross-correlation is even stronger, with a prediction potential up to two weeks, as we obtained $r = 0.87$ for $i = -1$ and still highly correlated $r = 0.75$ for $i = -2$. Therefore, this correlation results demonstrates the potential of Twitter for early warning and outbreak detection.

Further, in the real world, it is important to note that it takes about a week for the reported figures to reach the national level, be collated, and be acted upon. Therefore, the real-time monitoring of the social network could provide warning up to two weeks earlier in the UK and three weeks in the United States, significantly enhancing the preparedness and response operation.

In the United States, similar results were found by Signorini, Segre, and Polgreen (2011), who evaluated user sentiment during the swine flu outbreak and compared this sentiment with the CDC's reported disease levels. The data collection in their project started in October 2009, thus missing on the first spike in the 2009 swine flu epidemics. While the authors use SVM for classification of tweets, the results in terms of early warning potential also indicate outbreak detection that is about two weeks earlier than that of PH agencies, thus confirming our own results.

However, for seasonal diseases, unlike the 2009 swine flu outbreak, where such a high interest and activity on social media from the public is unlikely to be seen, more robust methods are required to develop a system operating on all disease and conditions, improving sensitivity (a percentage of actual outbreaks correctly identified) and mainly specificity (a percentage of days with no outbreak correctly identified) and thus avoiding unnecessary false positives (incorrect outbreak alarm when there is no outbreak happening) that might occur with current solutions.

3. Twitter – Risk Communication and Health News Dissemination

In addition to the potential for early warning, Twitter is increasingly important for risk communication during public health emergencies.

Traditionally, risk communication was conducted using mainstream media – national TV, press, and radio – using a top-down approach led by public health authorities and ministries of health. In this regard, the 2009 swine flu pandemics were a major breakthrough – Duncan (2009) illustrated the spectrum of swine flu media coverage in the European Union, while a specific study to analyze risk perception and information seeking behavior during the 2009 pandemic was conducted in Germany (Walter et al., 2012). Twitter was also investigated in its role as health news disseminator (Kwak et al., 2010). Much computing research, such as by Kwak et al. (2010), focused on understanding how information cascades through the Twitter social network. However, a large number of followers does not guarantee that information will propagate through the network (Cha et al., 2010) – other factors such as timeliness, accuracy, and entertainment play import roles. Savage (2011) looked into making sense of the information appearing in Twitter.

In the medical domain, the problems are challenging as they are addressing personal health – for example, inaccuracy of self-diagnosis of influenza due to the media hype was illustrated by Jutel et al. (2011) in the case of the 2009 swine flu outbreak. However, reporting public health information on social media during outbreaks (rather than sharing self-diagnosis data) remains a little-researched topic – one of high importance due to the fast nature of information spread during emergencies, as our following case study will demonstrate.

3.1. *Twitter Spreads the News of the Pandemic – a Case Study*

In this section, we discuss a case study of the role of Twitter for promotion of online resources covering the WHO's decision to increase the stage of the epidemic to 6^3 and declare a global "pandemic" on June 11, 2009. This was undoubtedly the most important event during the 2009 swine flu outbreak that, unsurprisingly, received widespread media attention and was extensively discussed on social media. After the WHO declaration of a pandemic state, a huge volume of information was published by online media with much focus on the effectiveness of vaccination programs and the possible methods to curb the spread of infection (Szomszor, Kostkova, & St. Louis, 2011).

Before we analyze the Twitter coverage of the pandemic, we briefly look at media dissemination through Twitter during the period before and after the declaration. A significant portion of the Twitter traffic we sampled contained a URL. Since the sample we have collected is focused on a particular topic (i.e., "flu"), the links posted provide a good indication of what resources are considered important by the community.

We conducted a classification of the most popular web resources found in our sample dataset to find out what types of resource are the most popular. A complete index of all hyperlinks appearing in our dataset posted to Twitter

---

[3]   http://www.who.int/csr/disease/swineflu/frequently_asked_questions/levels_pandemic_alert/en/.

Table 5.1. Categories of flu-related resources posted to Twitter
from June 2, 2009 to August 29, 2009

Category	Total Authors	Total Resources
Blog	7573	162
News	6151	117
Medical Organisation	4388	38
Spam	4231	312
Video	3897	72
Poll	741	5
Comic	484	8
Aggregator	318	10
Game	294	4
Sales	288	31
Download	248	8
Campaign	63	1
Suspended Account	5	1

was constructed, including the total number of times the URL appears as well
as the total number of distinct authors. For example, the three most popular
URLs were the following:

1. http://www.theonion.com/articles/obamas-declaration-of-swine-
   fluemergency-prompts,6952/, tweeted by 547 authors
2. http://www.benckenstein.com/digital-media/swine-flu-susan-boyleand
   -the-network-multiplier-effect/, tweeted by 468 authors
3. http://mashable.com/2009/11/10/google-flu-shot-map/, tweeted by 319
   authors

Note that the most popular was "coverage" by the satirical news site the *Onion*.
The classification task was conducted by an experienced journalism grad-stu-
dent on the most popular 769 resources posted between June 2, 2009, and
August 29, 2009, placing each item in one of the following categories: Blog,
News, Medical Organisation, Spam, Video, Poll, Comic, Aggregator, Game,
Sales, Download, Campaign, or Suspended Account.

Table 5.1 contains the total number of distinct authors and total number
of resources for each classification category. The most widely represented in
terms of number of distinct resources linked is spam (40 percent). In the majority of cases, this was simple to verify because the user's Twitter account had

been suspended or the redirection link registered with URL shortening services had been disabled.

We also identified the number of distinct authors who tweeted a reference to a resource (hence providing a direct measure of the resource's popularity). Blogs are the most widely linked (26 percent), closely followed by official news articles (21 percent) and pages from official medical organizations (15 percent).

Coming back to investigating the dissemination of the WHO decision to declare a global pandemic on June 11, 2009, a significant amount of reaction was captured by Twitter. This event and the corresponding data we have collected provide a unique opportunity to investigate how accurate and timely the responses from major news and public health organizations was, as well as how the news propagated through the network over time.

All links found in our sample dataset on the June 11 and 12, 2009, were examined. URLs were programmatically harvested to determine whether they are still active (i.e., they have not been disabled because they were spam) and whether they are redirected via a URL shortening service. After following all redirection links, it became apparent that many popular online news websites have more than one URL for a particular article. For example, extra arguments are often added to the URL, such as the search term used by the user to reach the page or localization information. Each resource was inspected manually to determine whether it was a direct reference to the WHO announcement. Articles from the most popular news organizations (both UK and U.S.) were shortlisted, along with those from two official health agencies: the WHO and the CDC.

Figure 5.4 shows the popularity of links posted to Twitter (in terms of the number of distinct authors) on an hour-by-hour basis twenty-four hours after the announcement (the time zone is GMT). Ultimately, the most popular resource is the BBC article (arriving to Twitter at 2–3 PM GMT), but this is not the first to make an appearance in Twitter. CNN, Reuters, and USA Today were the first to arrive in Twitter (10–11 AM GMT) – four hours before the BBC article was picked up. Both the WHO and CDC also have articles that appear in Twitter (the CDC's arriving much sooner than the WHO's), but their uptake is very small compared to the BBC and CNN articles. A link to the website of the European Centre for Disease Prevention and Control (ECDC) covering the news appeared only once.

To summarize, within the space of a few hours, most major news organizations had published on the topic, and those articles were propagated through Twitter. It would seem that timeliness is not a good predictor of overall success of dissemination of the news: between June 11 and 12, 2009, the BBC article

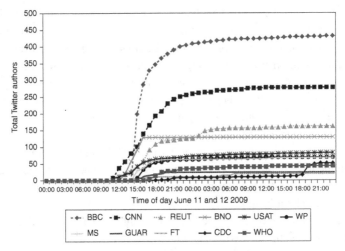

Figure 5.4. Hour-by-hour breakdown of the most popular resources posted to Twitter from the major news organizations and public health agencies when the WHO announced H1N1 was pandemic.

became the most popular even though it appeared on Twitter four hours later than other news agencies.

However, to fully incorporate social median channel in risk communication strategies by major public health agencies, more research is required to better understand public understanding, reaction, and behavior in response to emergency alerts. Also, the population not using social media and the Internet needs to continue being served by traditional mass media communications.

4. Twitter – Health Sentiment and Public Language

Twitter has been used to assess the populations' sentiment since the early days of Twitter research. For example, Golder et al. (2011) used Twitter to assess diurnal and seasonal mood across different cultures. Covering Twitter-based research into sentiment in general terms is not the aim of this chapter. Here we will focus on health sentiment; positive and negative feelings about diseases; and, in our case study, an important public health measure – vaccination.

The homophily hypothesis stipulates that social interactions and networks are a result of likeminded views and values, while according to social influence hypothesis, the causality is the other way around. A number of studies investigated the confounding of influence-driven and homophily-driven contagion in social networks; examples include Aral et al. (2009), Shalizi and Thomas (2011), among others. However, these factors have a wider implication for public health interventions, prevention measures, and disease control. Salathé et al. (2013) demonstrated that a large number of opinionated neighbors inhibit the expression of sentiments, while exposure to negative sentiment "spreads" and is predictive of future negative sentiment expression. On the other hand, exposure to positive sentiments is generally not; it can even predict increased negative sentiment expression.

An increasingly important role of Twitter also lies in providing an insight into public information needs; public understanding of health terminology; use of lay language, colloquial terms, and jargon; and the general information the public needs about health.

In a recent study of antibiotic understanding on Twitter, social media was shown to be a useful way to disseminate medical information, but that it is also prone to abuse (Scanfeld, Scanfeld, & Larson, 2010). In particular, Twitter can be used to assess public knowledge (e.g., the widely held but incorrect assumption that antibiotics will treat a cold, or that course of antibiotics, prescribed by a doctor, can be stopped once the symptoms have disappeared) and therefore reveal gaps in public understanding. Further, data correlation of three datasets (news, searches by public, and searches by professionals) were investigated on the NeLI/NRIC[4] datasets (Kostkova et al., 2013). Although this study did not use Twitter, it illustrated a strong correlation of public information needs with media coverage of health topics. Gesualdo et al. (2014) investigated the public usage of jargon in relation to ILI and correlated the use of related terms on Twitter, joining the ECDC ILI case definition with that of the United States' traditional surveillance systems.

Our case study illustrates the role of health sentiment on social networks regarding one of the most important public health measures, vaccination.

4.1. *Twitter Gets You Vaccinated: A Case Study*

Vaccination is an ideal example of successful public health intervention protecting entire populations from previously deadly communicable diseases (CDC, 1999). However, due to recent vaccination scares and antivaccination campaigns, previously high vaccination levels have been going down, and almost eradicated diseases (tuberculosis, measles, etc.) are on the rise (Ash, 2010). Outbreaks of vaccine preventable diseases (VPD) are more likely to

---

[4] www.neli.org.uk and www.nric.org.uk.

happen if overall vaccination rates decline (Jansen et al., 2003) or if a strong vaccination refusal is common in local communities.

Salathé and Khandelwal (2011) conducted a large investigation of vaccination sentiments in online social networks. Using publicly available data from 101,853 users of online media collected over a period of six months (from August 2009 until January 2010 in the United States) during the swine flu pandemics, a spatiotemporal sentiment toward a new vaccine was measured. This was validated against the CDC-estimated vaccination rates by region to demonstrate a strong correlation.

Out of the 477,768 collected tweets, 318,379 were classified relevant to the A(H1N1) vaccine. Tweets were classified into four categories: out of those 318,379 tweets, 255,828 were classified as "negative" and 35,884 as "positive," while the rest were considered "neutral" and "irrelevant." For example:

- "Off to get swine flu vaccinated before work" is a "positive" tweet.
- "What Can You Do to Resist the U.S. H1N1 'Vaccination' Program? Help Get Word Out. The H1N1 'Vaccine' Is DIRTY. DontGetIt," is a negative tweet.
- "The Health Department will be offering the seasonal flu vaccine for children 6 months–19 yrs. of age starting on Monday, Nov. 16," is deemed a "neutral" tweet.
- A tweet was labeled as "irrelevant" if it was retrieved in error and was not related to vaccination and swine flu.

Three machine learning classification algorithms were used (Naïve Bayes, Maximum Entropy, and a Dynamic Language Model classifier), and labels to train the classifiers were provided by students participating in the study, demonstrating 64 percent average accuracy. A social network was created from the data by taking into account all users (constituting "nodes") who posted at least one positive, negative, or neutral tweet. An "edge" in the social network (SN) between users A or B means that A was B's follower at any point of time or vice versa. Note that this algorithm treats the network as static rather than as dynamic. The overall influenza vaccine sentiment score is defined as the relative difference of positive and negative tweets ($(n_+ - n_-)/(n_+ + n_- + n_0)$).

Figure 5.5a shows the absolute numbers of positive, negative, and neutral tweets per day in the United States. The overall influenza vaccine sentiment score started at a negative value in late summer 2009, but showed large short-term fluctuations. The fourteen-day moving average turned positive in mid-October 2009 (as the vaccine became available) and remained positive for the rest of the year (see Figure 5.5b). The influenza A(H1N1) vaccination sentiment score was found positive, correlated with estimated vaccination coverage as provided by CDC. The authors found a very strong correlation on

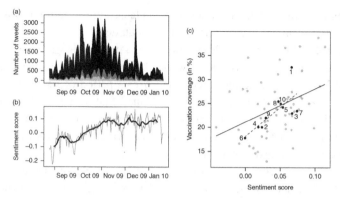

Figure 5.5 (a) Total number of negative (bottom region), positive (middle region), and neutral (top region) tweets relating to the influenza A(H1N1) vaccination during the fall wave of the 2009 pandemic. (b) Daily (fluctuating line) and fourteen-day moving average (thick line) sentiment scores during the same time. (c) Correlation between estimated vaccination rates for individuals older than six months and sentiment score per HHS region (dark dots) and states (light dots). Numbers represent the ten regions as defined by the U.S. Department of Human Health and Services. Lines shows best fit of linear regression (short line for regions, long line for states).
Salathé and Khandelwal (2011).

the level of U.S. Department of Health and Human Services (HHS) regions (weighted $r = 0.78$, $p = 0.017$) using the estimated vaccination coverage for all persons older than six months (see Figure 5.5c), as well as a strong correlation at the state level (weighted $r = 0.52$, $p = 0.0046$).These results are important for planning public health efforts focusing on target areas for communication interventions.

5. Discussion

5.1. *User Demographics*

Firstly, Twitter is creating bias due to lack of representativeness of the population demographics. Pew Research Center investigating Twitter usage in America revealed that Internet users aged eighteen to twenty-nine are significantly more likely to use Twitter than older adults and that minority (African American and Latino) Internet users are more than twice as likely to tweet as white Internet users.[5] Furthermore, women (10 percent) are using the service more actively than men (7 percent). Personal information dominates

---

[5]   http://www.pewinternet.org/Reports/2010/Twitter-Update-2010.aspx.

the communication (72 percent), closely followed by work communication (62 percent). The Pew Research Center also found that 31 percent of users used their mobile phones to search information about their health,[6] which has almost doubled since Pew's previous study in 2010 when it was 17 percent of users (Fox, 2009). Relying on the dramatic increase of Twitter usage globally, demographic bias is unlikely to be a major issue for Twitter research in the future; however, in comparison with the randomized control trials (RCT) widely used for epidemiological studies, the digital divide bias needs to be considered when Twitter dataset results are to be generalized.

5.2. *Location Awareness*

Further, location awareness remains an issue; reliance on profile variables is introducing an inevitable bias, while the availability of Global Positioning System (GPS) coordinates of tweets, providing the desirable accuracy and location awareness, is still in a far future from a global users' perspective. Other methods for determining user location beyond GPS are discussed in Chapter 1.

5.3. *Integration of Multiple Data Sources*

Barboza et al. (2013) compared operational early warning systems on a detection of A/H5N1 influenza events. They highlighted the need for "more efficient synergies and cross-fertilization of knowledge and information" (Barboza et al., 2013, p. 8). A roadmap for digital disease surveillance that incorporated new data sources was also outlined (Kostkova, 2013) and identified six types of data sources:

- *News/online media* (including automated scanning systems such as MediSys (Linge et al., 2009))
- *Digital traces* (such as the online keyword searches researched by Ginsberg et al. (2008) and Wiseman et al. (2010))
- *Pro-Med* (a professional mailing list for communicable diseases[7])
- *Labs/clinical reports*
- *Participatory systems* (such as the multilingual EpiWorks project Influenzanet[8] and the UK portal Flusurvey[9])
- *Twitter/social media*

---

[6] http://mhealthwatch.com/infographic-how-are-medical-professionals-using-social-media-20981/.
[7] http://www.promedmail.org/.
[8] http://www.influenzanet.eu/.
[9] http://flusurvey.org.uk/.

Integration efforts combining all social media, participatory systems, and traditional surveillance to enhance the early warning capacity and rapid response by public health agencies are under way under the *medi+board* framework dashboard (Kostkova et al., 2014a, 2014b), but these efforts will require further research, health stakeholder engagement, and political will.

Twitter inevitably has the potential to spread evidence-based information quickly. However, how to use this potential effectively in public health emergencies to best protect the public from relying on distorted and panic-raising coverage remains a challenge.

5.4. *Twitter – Personalized Health Information and Privacy*

Undoubtedly, Twitter has huge potential to deliver personalized targeted information to users where and when they need it. Even better, using geo-tagging, it can direct those in need to local healthcare services and professional health advice in their vicinity. This opportunity brings major ethical challenges for privacy and personal data usage that have not been widely researched yet.

This closely relates to user privacy – while Twitter users agree to sharing their information in the public domain, which enables an unprecedented amount of research data to be available for research, not all users seem fully aware of this fact. Further, it goes without saying that Twitter is not the most appropriate media for sharing sensitive personal health information nor for providing personalized advice. Striking the right balance between user privacy and health advice opportunities is an ongoing challenge. While there are public reservations about governments' attempts to share electronic patients records (EPR) for research benefits and/or commercial needs (for example, the controversial Care. Data initiative in the UK in 2014), the popularity of MedTech wearable and tracking devices resulted in users being increasingly willing to give up their private personal health data (often with GPS location coordinates) to the industry without any control of the usage, sharing, or even sale. These ethical challenges require further open debate with all major stakeholders, including users, citizens, healthcare providers, governments, researchers, IT, and MedTech industry to ensure that the right balance is agreed upon and enforced.

References

Aral, Muchnik. L. and Sundararajan, A. (2009). Distinguishing influence-based contagion from homophily-driven diffusion in dynamic networks. *Proceedings of National Academy of Science USA*, 106, 21544–9.

Ash, C. (2010). Summun bonum. *Science Translations Medicine*, 2 (61) ed8.

Balcan, D., Hu, H., Goncalves, B., Bajardi, P., Poletto, C., Ramasco, J. J., Paolotti, D., Perra, N., Tizzoni, M., Van Den Broeck, W., Colizza, V., and Vespignani, A. (2009). Seasonal transmission potential and activity peaks of the influenza A(H1N1): a Monte Carlo likelihood analysis based on human mobility. *BMC Medicine*, 7, 45 doi: 10.1186/1741-7015-7-45.

Barboza, P., Vaillant, L., Mawudeku, A., Nelson, N. P., Hartley, D. M., Madoff, L. C., Linge, J. P., Collier, N., Brownstein, J. S., Yangarber, R., and Astagneu, P. (2013). Evaluation of epidemic intelligence systems integrated in the earl alert in and reporting project of the detection of A/H5N1 influenza events. *PLOS ONE*, 8(3), e57272.

Centers for Disease Control and Prevention (CDC). (1999). Ten great public health achievements – United States. 1900–1999. *MMWR Morbidity Mortality Weekly Report*, 48, 241–3.

Cha, M., Haddadi, H., Benevenuto, F. and Gummadi, K. P. (2010). Measuring user influence in Twitter: the million follower fallacy. In *Proceedings of the International AAAI Conference on Weblogs and Social Media (ICWSM)*, Association for the Advancement of Artificial Intelligence (www.aaai.org). http://snap.stanford.edu/class/cs224w-readings/cha10influence.pdf

Christakis, N. A., and Fowler, J. H. (2007). The spread of obesity in a large social network over 32 years. *New England Journal of Medicine*, 357, 370–9.

Christakis, N. A, and Fowler, J. H. (2008). The collective dynamics of smoking in a large scale social network. *New England Journal of Medicine*, 358, 2249–58.

Culotta, A. (2010.) Towards detecting influenza epidemics by analyzing Twitter messages. In *ACM, Proceedings of the SOMA '10* (pp. 115–22). ACM.

de Quincey, Ed, and Kostkova, Patty. (2010.) Early warning and outbreak detection using social networking websites: the potential of Twitter. In *ehealth 2009, Springer Lecture Notes of the Institute for Computer Sciences, Social-Informatics and Telecommunications Engineering (LNICST) 27*, ed. P. Kostkova (pp. 21–4). Springer Verlag.

de Quincey, E., Kyriacou, T., Williams, N., and Pantin, T. (2014). Potential of social media to determine hay fever seasons and drug efficacy. *Planet@Risk* 2(4, Special Issue on One Health): 293–7.

Duncan, B. (2009). How the media reported the first day of the pandemic H1N1 2009: results of EU-wide media analysis. *Eurosurveillance*, 14(30): 1–3. http://www.eurosurveillance.org/images/dynamic/EE/V14N30/art19286.pdf.

Fox, S. (2009). The social life of health information. Available at http://www.pewinternet.org/Reports/2009/8-The-Social-Life-of-Health-Information/14-About-Us-Methodology.aspx?view=all.

Ginsberg, J., Mohebbi, M. H., Patel, R. S., Brammer, L., Smolinski, M. S., and Brilliant, L. (2008). Detecting influenza epidemics using search engine query data. *Nature*, 457, 10.1038/nature07634.

Golder, Scott A., et al. (2011). Diurnal and seasonal mood vary with work, sleep, and daylength across different cultures. *Science*, 333, 1878 doi: 10.1126/science.1202775.

Gomide, J., Veloso, A., Meira, W., Jr., Almeida, V., Benevenuto, F., Ferraz, F., and Teixeira, M. (2011.) Dengue surveillance based on a computational model of spatio-temporal locality of Twitter. In *ACM, Web Science 2011* (pp. 1–8). ACM.

Gesualdo, F. Stilo, G., Agricola, E., Gonfiantini, M. V., Pandolfi, E., Velardi, P., and Tozzi, A. E. (2014). Influenza-like illness surveillance on Twitter through automated learning of naive language. *PLOS ONE*, 8(12), e82489.

Hay, S. I., George, D. B., Moyer, C. L., and Brownstein, J. S. (2013). Big data opportunities for global infectious disease surveillance. *PLOS Medicine*, 10(4), e1001413.

Jansen, V. A. A., et al. (2003). Measles outbreaks in a population with declining vaccine update. *Science*, 301, 804.

Jutel, A., Baker, M. G., Stanley, J., Huang, Q. S., and Bandaranayake, D. (2011). Self-diagnosis of influenza during a pandemic: a cross-sectional survey. *BMJ Open*, 1:e000234. dio:10.1136/bjmopen-2011-000234.

Kaiser, R., and Coulombier, D. (2006). Different approaches to gathering epidemic intelligence in Europe. *Eurosurveillance*, 11(17), pii=2948.

Kaiser, R. Coulombier, D., Maldari, M., Morgan, D., and Paquet, C. (2006). What is epidemic intelligence, and how it is being improved in Europe? *Eurosureillance*, 11(2), 060202.

Kostkova, P. (2013). A roadmap to integrated digital public health surveillance: the vision and the challenges. In *Proceedings of the 22nd International Conference on World Wide Web Companion (WWW '13 Companion)* (pp. 687–94). International World Wide Web Conferences Steering Committee.

Kostkova, P. Fowler, D., Wiseman, S., and Weinberg, J. R. (2013). Major infection events over 5 years: how is media coverage influencing online information needs of health care professionals and the public? *Journal of Medical Internet Research (JMIR)*, 15(7), e107 doi:10.2196/jmir.2146.

Kostkova, P., Garbin, S., Moser, J., and Pan, W. (2014a) Integration and visualization public health dashboard: the *medi+board* pilot project. In *Proceedings of the Companion Publication of the 23rd International Conference on World Wide Web Companion (WWW '14 Companion)* doi: 10.1145/2567948.2579276. International World Wide Web Conferences Steering Committee.

Kostkova, P. (2014b) *Medi+ board*: the Public Health Dashboard. Medicine 2.0 Conference 2014, October 2014, JMIR Publications Inc. Canada.

Kostkova, P., Szomszor, M., and St Luis, C. (2014). #swineflu: the use of Twitter as an early warning and risk communication tool in the 2009 swine flu pandemic. *ACM Transactions on Management Information Systems*, 5(2), Article 8.

Kostkova, P. (2015). Grand Challenges in Digital Health. *Frontiers in Public Health: Digital Health.* Frontiers.

Kwak, H., Lee, C., Park, H., and Moon, S. (2010.) "What is Twitter, a social network or a news media?" In *Proceedings of the 19th International Conference on World Wide Web (WWW2010)* (pp. 591–600). ACM.

Lampos, V., and Cristianini, N. (2010.) "Tracking the flu pandemic by monitoring the social web." In *Proceedings of the 2nd IAPR Workshop on Cognitive Information Processing (CIP2010)* (pp. 411–16). IEEE Press.

Lampos, V., and Cristianini, N. (2012). Nowcasting events from the social web with statistical learning. *ACM TISM*, 3(4), Article 72.

Lampos, V., de Bie, T., and Cristianini, N. (2010). "Flu detector – tracking epidemics on Twitter." In *Proceedings of the European Conference on Machine Learning* and Principles and Practice of Knowledge Discovery in Databases (ECML PKDD 2010) (pp. 599–602). Springer.

Linge, J. P, Steinberger, R., Weber, T. P., Yangarber, R., van der Goot, E., Al Khudhairy, D. H., and Stilianakis, N. I. (2009). Internet surveillance systems for early alerting of health threats. EuroSurveillance, 14(13), pii=1916.

Malik. S. (2011.) Which idea is likely to make the biggest impact on healthcare by 2020? BMJ, 342: d1998 doi: 10.1136/bmj.d1998.

Paquet C., Coulombier, D., Kaiser, R., and Ciotti, M. (2006). Epidemic intelligence: a new framework for strengthening disease surveillance in Europe. Eurosurveillance 11(12), p=665.

Paul, M. J., and Dredze, M. (2011). You and what you tweet: analyzing Twitter or public health. In The Proceedings of the 5th AAAI Conference on Weblogs and Social Media. (pp. 265–72). AAAI.

Sadilek, A., and Kautz, H. (2013). Modeling the impact of lifestyle on health at scale. In Sixth ACM International Conference on Web Search and Data Mining (WSDM) (pp. 637–46). ACM.

Salathé, M., et al. (2012). Digital epidemiology. PLoS Computational Biology, 8(7), e1002616. dio:10.1371/journal.pcbi.1002616.

Salathé, M., Duy, Q. V., Shashank, K., and Hunter, D. R. (2013). The dynamics of health behaviour sentiments on a large online social network. EPJ Data Science, 2, 4.

Salathé, M., Freifeld, C. C., Mekaru, S. R., Tomasulo, A. F., and Brownstein, J. S. (2013). Influenza A (H7N9) and the importance of digital epidemiology. New England Journal of Medicine (July 3), nwjm.org.

Salathé, M., and Khandelwal, S. (2011). Assessing vaccination sentiments with online social media: implications for infectious disease dynamics and control. PLOS Computational Biology, 7(10), e1002199.

Savage, N. (2011). Twitter as medium and message. Communications of the ACM, 54(3), 8–20.

Scanfeld, D., Scanfeld, V., and Larson, E. L. (2010). Dissemination of health information through social networks: Twitter and antibiotics. AJIC: American Journal of Infection Control, 3(8), 182–8.

Shalizi, C. R., and Thomas, A. C. (2011). Homophily and contagion are generically confounded in observational social network studies. Sociology Methods Research, 40, 211–39.

Signorini, A., Segre, A. M., and Polgreen, P. M. (2011). The use of Twitter to track levels of disease activity and public health concern in the U.S. during the influenza A H1N1 pandemic. POS One, 6(5), e19467 doi: 10.1371/journal.pone.0019467.

Smith, K. P., and Christakis, N. A. (2008). Social networks and health. Annual Review of Sociology, 34, 405–29.

St. Louis, C., and Zorlu, G. (2012). Can Twitter predict disease outbreaks? BMJ, 344, e2353. Available online at http://www.bmj.com/content/344/bmj.e2353.

Szomszor, M., Kostkova, P., and de Quincey, E. (2011). #swineflu: Twitter predicts swine flu outbreak in 2009. In ehealth 2010, Springer Lecture Notes of the Institute far Computer Sciences, Social-Informatics and Telecommunications Engineering (LNICST) 69, eds. M. Szomszor and P. Kostkova (pp. 18–26). Springer.

Szomszor, M., Kostkova, P., and St. Louis, C. (2011). Twitter informatics: tracking and understanding public reaction during the 2009 swine flu pandemics. In *IEEE/ WIC/ACM International Conferences on Web Intelligence and Intelligent Agent Technology, WI-IAT*, vol. 1 (pp. 320–3). IEEE.

Takahashi, T., Abe, S., and Igata, N. (2011). Can Twitter be an alternative of real-world sensors? *Lecture Notes in Computer Science*, 6763, 240–9.

Valente, T. W. (2010). *Social Networks and Health*. Oxford University Press.

Walter, D., Bohmer, M. M., Reiter, S., Krause, G., and Wichmann, O. (2012). Risk perception and information-seeking behaviour during the 2009–10 influenza A (H1N1) PDM09 pandemic in Germany. *Eurosurveillance*, 7(13), 1–8.

Wiseman, S., Kostkova, P., de Quincey, E., and Jawaheer, G. (2010). Providing guidance during the swine flu outbreak in 2009: an evaluation study of the National Resource for Infection Control (NRIC). Poster and abstract in *The Proceedings of the 14th International Conference on Infectious Diseases (ICID)* (p. e105). Elsevier.

6

Disaster Monitoring

Bella Robinson, Robert Power, and Mark Cameron

Twitter is a new data channel for emergency managers to source public information for situational awareness and as a means of engaging with the community during disaster response and recovery activities. Twitter has been used successfully to identify emergency events, obtain crowdsourced information as the event unfolds, provide up-to-date information to the affected community from authoritative agencies, and conduct resource planning.

1. Introduction

1.1. *Motivation*

Natural disasters have increased in severity and frequency in recent years. According to Guha-Sapir et al. (2011), in 2010, 385 natural disasters killed over 297,000 people worldwide, impacted 217 million human lives, and cost the global economy an estimated US$123.9 billion. There are numerous examples from around the world: the 2004 Indian Ocean earthquake and tsunami; the more recent 2011 Tōhoku earthquake and tsunami, which damaged the Fukushima nuclear power station; hurricanes Katrina and Sandy in 2005 and 2012 respectively; the 2010 China floods, which caused widespread devastation; and Victoria's 2009 "Black Saturday" bushfires in Australia, killing 173 people and having an estimated A$2.9 billion in total losses (Stephenson, Handmer, & Haywood, 2012).

This chapter presents case studies highlighting the use of Twitter together with a survey of existing tools and techniques.

With urban development occurring on coastlines and spreading into rural areas, houses and supporting infrastructure are expanding into high-risk regions. The growing world population is moving into areas progressively more prone to natural disasters and unpredictable weather events. These events have been increasing in frequency and severity in recent years (Hawkins et al., 2012).

It has been recognized that information published by the general public on social media is relevant to emergency managers and that social media is a useful means of providing information to communities that may be impacted by emergency events (Lindsay, 2011; Anderson, 2012). To prepare and respond to such emergency situations effectively, it is critical that emergency managers have relevant and reliable information. For example, bushfire management is typically a regional government responsibility, and each jurisdiction has its own agency that takes the lead in coordinating community preparedness and responding to bushfires when they occur. These agencies are responsible for firefighting activities, training to prepare communities to protect themselves, land management hazard reduction, as well as situations involving search and rescue.

During periods of high fire danger, these fire agencies continuously monitor weather conditions in preparation for responding to events when they occur. They also inform the community about known incidents.[1] These agencies also publish incident information on social media sites such as Facebook and Twitter.[2] This provides a new channel of communication to interact with the community to both provide information about known events and to receive crowdsourced content from the general public.

This engagement of social media is yet to be fully utilized. During crisis events, the emergency services effectively use social media to provide information to the community, but their ability to obtain information from the public is limited (Lindsay, 2011). While there are social media success stories – for example, the Queensland Police Service in Australia during the 2011 Brisbane Floods (Charlton, 2012), which is discussed in Section 2.6 – they are not yet widespread.

Consequently, emergency and disaster management is undergoing reform around the world. Disaster resilience will strengthen when government, business, communities, and individuals collectively adopt risk-based planning and mitigation strategies.

---

[1] http://www.rfs.nsw.gov.au/.
[2] See the examples http://www.facebook.com/nswrfs and https://twitter.com/NSWRFS.

In summary, the issues facing the emergency management sector involve decisions of where to best allocate investment across the prevention, preparedness, response, and recovery (PPRR) spectrum to increase community safety and reduce the costs and social effects of emergencies and disasters. This can be achieved by improving the quality, availability, and management of data and will include information sourced from social media in near-real time. The challenges are many, the most significant being how to reliably extract relevant information about emergency events of interest for crisis coordinators. The survey of existing tools and technologies and the case studies described in this chapter demonstrate that Twitter is an effective source of public information for situational awareness for emergency managers and crisis coordinators and is also a useful means of engaging with the community during disaster response and recovery activities.

1.2. *The Disaster Lifecycle*

Emergency management operates in a context where policies and practice contribute to the goal of a *safer, sustainable community* so that citizens can live, work, and pursue their needs and interests in a safe and sustainable physical and social environment. The risk to a *safer, sustainable community* from emergencies and disasters lies in the interactions between *hazards* to which a community is exposed and the *vulnerability* of the community's environment, physical, emotional, social, and economic infrastructure to such exposure. Levels of vulnerability range from complete *susceptibility* to complete *resilience*.

In a comprehensive approach to emergency management encompassing all hazards, there are four types of activities that contribute to the reduction or elimination of hazards and to reducing the susceptibility or increasing the resilience to hazards of a community or environment.

These activities are *prevention/mitigation activities*, which seek to eliminate or reduce the impact of hazards and/or move the susceptibility of a community subject to hazard impacts toward a more resilient foundation; *preparedness activities*, which prepare the community to deal effectively with emergencies and disasters through education material, information awareness, and emergency management arrangements and plans; *response activities*, which activate preparedness arrangements and plans to mobilize response resources to deal effectively with the emergency or disaster situation; and *recovery activities*, which assist an impacted community with reconstruction of the physical infrastructure and restoration of emotional, social, and economic well-being. The activities are not strictly linear and are shown in Figure 6.1.

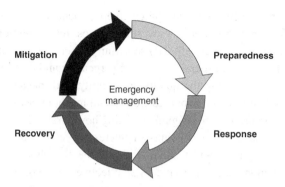

Figure 6.1. The PPRR life cycle.
http://www.stpaul.gov/index.aspx?nid=97.

1.3. *Managing Emergencies and Disasters*

Considerable coordination of national, state/territory, local governments, utilities, commercial, and voluntary organizations across the PPRR spectrum of activities is needed to realize the goal of an integrated and effective emergency management enterprise for every community.

National governments in most developed countries operate crisis command facilities to monitor all-hazards 24/7 to provide whole-of-government situation awareness for high-level decision making. These facilities typically coordinate information flows across government agencies and help manage the government's response to concurrent domestic crises and provide support during international incidents. The four main functions of these facilities are *situation awareness, intelligence, planning*, and *public communication.*

Coordination arrangements are well documented in emergency management plans that set out the planning and policy framework, roles, and responsibilities and coordination arrangements of agencies participating in the various emergency management enterprises. These emergency management plans outline who the front-line agencies are for specific events and define their tasks and lines of command.

These plans normally consist of at least five functional elements to manage an incident or emergency: control unit; planning unit; operations unit; logistics unit; and public information unit. The public information unit has been a recent addition to the incident management team structure and functions.

Within this emergency management structure, the control unit is responsible for management of activities to resolve an incident. The planning unit collects and analyzes information and develops plans to resolve incidents. The logistics unit coordinates the supply chain for resources needed to address an incident. The operations support unit tasks people and resources to deal with activities relevant to an incident. The public information unit provides warnings, information, and advice to affected communities, media, and the public.

Social media is a new channel for communicating information to (potentially impacted) communities as well as a channel for receiving community-based intelligence about local conditions. The potential for social media to improve the situation awareness of incident management teams for large-scale incident management is enormous.

1.4. *Situation Awareness*

Situation awareness, as originally defined by Endsley (1995, p. 36), involves "the perception of elements in the environment within a volume of time and space, the comprehension of their meaning, and the projection of their status in the near future." Building situation awareness in a given environment rests on being able to identify an appropriate set of perception elements, coupled with higher-level comprehension patterns/templates and forecast operators. While originally surfacing as a concept in the military domain, situation awareness is relevant across a wide range of domains for both individual and team activities. Situation awareness has been recognized as a critical part of making successful and effective decisions for emergency response.

Situation awareness itself has three levels: level 1 (Perception); level 2 (Comprehension); and level 3 (Projection). Perception is about picking up sensory cues from the environment. Comprehension involves combining sensory cues and interpreting the information. Projection deals with forecasting what might happen next.

Understanding a situation rests on identifying an appropriate set of perception elements, higher-level comprehension patterns/templates, and forecast operators. A situation awareness system understands its environment at multiple levels: from the Perception of events in raw data streams, to Comprehension of situations, through to Projection (or prediction) of likely futures (Endsley, 1995). Maintaining situation awareness of an incident allows watch officers to effectively plan and implement responses and anticipate and manage requests for information about incidents.

1.5. *Current Systems*

The need for timely information from social media for the purposes of disaster and emergency management is recognized internationally. A number of tools and systems have been developed over recent years to help emergency managers find and make use of the valuable information that is posted on Twitter by the public during an emergency event. These tools aim to improve the situational awareness of events as they unfold.

Twitcident (Abel et al., 2012)[3] performs real-time monitoring of Twitter messages to increase safety and security. They target large gatherings of people for purposes of crowd management, such as illegal parties, riots, and organized celebrations. Their tool is adjustable to specific locations and incident types, relying on official sources for event detection.

The system is activated when an incident notification is received. It first profiles the incident, setting location, incident type, and keywords. Incident profiles are continuously updated to adapt to topic changes that arise within an incident. Tweets that match this profile are then collected via the REST and Streaming Twitter APIs. They then perform named entity extraction (NER) to identify entities such as people, locations, or organizations that are mentioned within the tweets. They make use of four different NER services for this: DBpedia Spotlight,[4] AlchemyAPI,[5] OpenCalais,[6] and Zemanta.[7] The extracted entities are then mapped to concepts in DBpedia.[8]

An example screenshot of Twitcident is shown in Figure 6.2. A faceted search interface is provided on the left that allows the user to further filter the tweets displayed in the center portion of the screen. The system also produces some real-time analytics charts to provide an overview of how people are responding to the incident on Twitter.

Twitcident performs classification, using handcrafted rules, to identify tweets that are reports about casualties, infrastructure damage, or risks. The classification process also attempts to determine whether the tweeter is seeing, feeling, hearing, or smelling something. Hyperlinks contained within the tweet message are then examined, where the main content of the linked page is extracted using Boilerpipe[9] and then put through the NER module to identify more named entities. Keyword- or semantic-based filtering techniques are then applied to identify the tweets that are relevant to the incident.

Tweet4act (Chowdhury et al., 2013) uses keyword methods to retrieve tweets related to a crisis situation. Text classification techniques are then applied to assign those tweets automatically to pre-incident, during-incident,

---

[3] http://twitcident.org/.
[4] https://github.com/dbpedia-spotlight/dbpedia-spotlight/wiki.
[5] http://alchemyapi.com.
[6] http://opencalais.com.
[7] http://www.zemanta.com/.
[8] http://dbpedia.org.
[9] https://code.google.com/p/boilerpipe/.

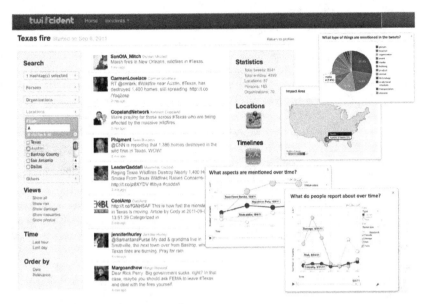

Figure 6.2. Twitcident screenshot.
Abel et al. (2012).

and post-incident classes. Other research (Imran et al., 2013) has used machine learning techniques to map tweets related to a crisis situation into classes defined in a disaster-related ontology to find informative tweets that contribute to situational awareness.

Another approach (Schulz & Ristoski, 2013; Schulz, Ristoski, & Paulheim, 2013) for real-time identification of small-scale incidents using microblogs combines information from the social and the semantic web. They define a machine learning algorithm combining text classification and semantic enrichment of microblogs using Linked Open Data. Their approach has been applied to detect three classes of small-scale incident: car, fire, and shooting.

The Emergency Situation Awareness (ESA)[10] system (Cameron et al., 2012) provides all-hazard situation awareness information for emergency managers using content gathered from the public Twitter API. New tweets from specific regions of interest are retrieved every 20 seconds via the Search API using geographic query constraints. This enables ESA to gather all geolocatable tweets from Australia and New Zealand. Tweets are geolocatable if they are either geotagged or have a user profile location set. These tweets are filtered and analyzed in near-real time, enabling alerting for unexpected incidents and monitoring of emergency events with results accessible via an interactive website.

[10] https://esa.csiro.au.

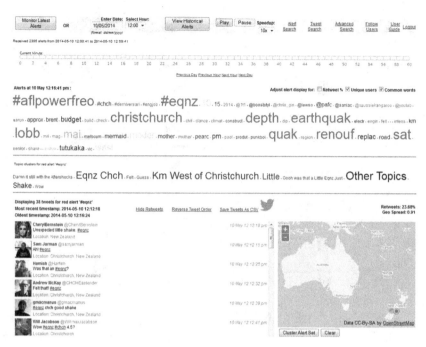

Figure 6.3. Emergency Situation Awareness.

Using a background language model, a burst detection module is able to generate alerts for unusually high-frequency words. These alerts are presented as a tag cloud in the interface, as shown in Figure 6.3, which shows the detection of an earthquake event. From the alert tag cloud, users can then drill down to get cluster summaries for a selected alert and view the contributing individual tweets. A heatmap provides a geographic indication of the location from which the tweets contributing to the alert originated. As well as monitoring for the current alerts, ESA allows the user to go back in time and replay alerts that were generated in the past. This is useful for post-event analysis. In addition to the all-hazard alert monitor functionality, ESA also has customized components that are especially tailored for detecting earthquake and fire events. These use text classification techniques to help determine whether a tweet containing specific keywords is a report of feeling an earthquake or is referring to an actual fire event and not some other use of the word "fire." ESA's event detection components are discussed further in Section 2.4.

CrisisTracker (Rogstadius et al., 2013) is an open source[11] online platform that extracts situation awareness by performing clustering of related tweets

[11] https://github.com/JakobRogstadius/CrisisTracker.

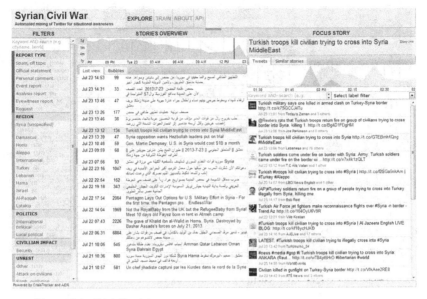

Figure 6.4. CrisisTracker.

to generate stories that are then analyzed and verified by volunteer curators. Tweets are gathered via the streaming API using a combination of geographic bounding box and keyword filters. During an eight-day trial of the system that focused on the Syrian Civil War in 2012, the platform's creators recruited forty-four volunteer curators. Curators' tasks involved initially examining the story clusters, possibly merging duplicates or removing irrelevant content, and then annotating each story with a geographic location and deployment-specific report categories (for example, infrastructure damage or violence) and identifying named entities. Stories that are determined to be irrelevant to the ongoing crisis can be hidden and so won't appear in future searches within the system. They found that on average a curator spent 4.5 minutes working on each story and worked 28.5 minutes per session before requiring a break of at least 15 minutes. In total, 3,600 annotation tags were added to 820 stories (1,775 before merging), and the total number of tweets belonging to stories was 616,009, which is substantial. Language issues were identified where some non-Arabic speaker curators were uncomfortable using automatic language translators to process Arabic content. These curators chose to focus solely on stories in their native language English. It was also noted that locations mentioned within English reports proved to be the most difficult to geolocate, as the translated location names often could not be found on the map. Figure 6.4 shows a

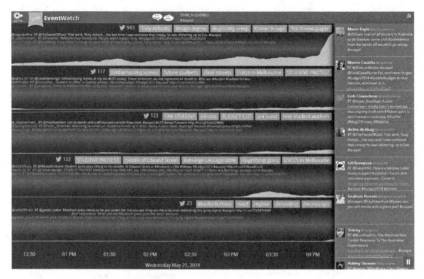

Figure 6.5. EventWatch Twitter monitoring tool.

screenshot of the CrisisTracker interface being used to examine tweets related to the Syrian Civil War.

While not specifically disaster-related, the EventWatch tool[12] can be configured to collect and analyze tweets related to a specific emergency event. As shown in Figure 6.5, tweets are collected and analyzed in near–real time. Tweet clustering is performed with the assistance of keyphrase extraction and named entity recognition techniques. Sentiment analysis can also be performed over each cluster.

2. Challenges

When monitoring Twitter to gain situation awareness during a disaster, there are several key issues that need to be addressed:

- **Volume:** There are too many tweets to read them all. Even when using simple keyword filters, finding tweets that contain valuable disaster-related information is difficult.
- **Location:** Automatically determining the place or location a tweet is referring to is difficult. Most tweets are not geotagged, and inferring location

---

[12] http://www.nicta.com.au/category/industry-engagement/broadband-and-the-digital-economy/projects/sentiment-analysis-tools..

from a tweeter's profile or the tweet message itself is problematic and is often done by hand. See Chapter 1 for more details.

- **Veracity:** Are the tweets trustworthy? During recent disasters – for example, Hurricane Sandy – false images and rumors were circulated. Identifying and myth-busting these tweets are important tasks for a disaster management agency.
- **Preparedness:** Some disaster events are known about ahead of time, for example, cyclones, fires, and floods, but others cannot be predicted, such as an earthquake or flash flooding. Is it possible to and reliably detect new events automatically?
- **Seek help:** When traditional emergency lines of communication, such as 911 in the United States, become unavailable, social media is increasingly seen as a viable alternative for people to seek help. How should emergency agencies respond to such requests?
- **Communication:** People use social media in times of crisis to find out information about the event, to seek help, to check whether their loved ones are okay, and to check the extent of damage that has occurred in the affected area. It is also used as a form of psychological first aid and for community resilience.

The following sections outline research activities that address these problems.

2.1. *Managing Tweet Volume*

Current disaster monitoring systems use a variety of ways to find and annotate disaster-related tweets. The Ushahidi platform[13] relies solely on human volunteers to manually examine each post and assign it to the correct category and location. This platform has been used successfully during the Haiti earthquake disaster (see Heinzelman & Waters, 2010), but it relies on the availability of a large group of volunteers. It was also used during the Hurricane Sandy event in 2012 for the District of Columbia (Washington, D.C.); see the example in Figure 6.6.

Often a large group of volunteer annotators is not available, so the use of a system that can automatically classify posts as being relevant to the disaster or not is highly appealing. It should be noted, however, that the overall accuracy of text classifiers will almost never be as good as a human annotator. Imran et al. (2014) propose a tweet classification system that is trained manually as a disaster unfolds. In this way, volunteers are presented with a small subset of

---

[13] http://www.ushahidi.com/product/ushahidi/.

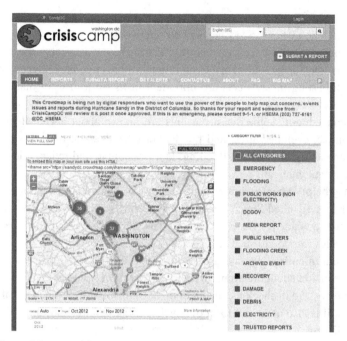

Figure 6.6. Ushahidi crowd map.
https://sandydc.crowdmap.com/.

tweets to label. The system then automatically classifies the remaining incoming tweets, thus significantly reducing the manual workload. The authors show that classifiers developed using data from other events perform poorly, which is in contrast to the research carried out by Verma et al. (2011), who found that classifiers trained on specific events performed well on other similar events. For example, a classifier trained on tweets from one flooding event was shown to perform well when tested on data from another flooding event.

Several text classification methods can be applied to the task of classifying tweets. Popular ones are Support Vector Machines (Joachims, 1998), Maximum Entropy (Nigam, Lafferty, & McCallum, 1999), Naive Bayes (Lewis, 1998), and Decision Tree (Lewis & Ringuette, 1994). All of these methods require preparation to train the classifier, which involves manually labeling a set of example tweets and experimenting with feature selection. Usually these example tweets correspond to positive and negative examples of the target subject. For example, the tweets may or may not be informative, or they may be examples from a number of different subject categories. Often, several human annotators carry out the same task, and only tweets where they all agree on the label are included in the final training set.

Once a training set is assembled, the next thing to do is determine the tweet features to train the classifier on. These are characteristics of the tweet that might be useful indicators as to which class it belongs. Some possible features include unigrams and bigrams (that is, the words within the tweet); the length of the tweet in characters; the number of words in the tweet; the presence and/ or number of hashtags; user mentions and hyperlinks; part of speech (POS) tags (noun, verb, and so on); the presence and/or number of particular characters or emoticons (for example, a question mark, exclamation mark, happy face, sad face); whether the tweet contains a first-, second-, or third-person pronoun; the number of uppercase characters; the number of positive/negative sentiment words; and retweet count. As an example, when classifying tweets to determine whether they were firsthand reports of feeling an earthquake, Robinson, Power, and Cameron (2013a) found that positive tweets are usually short, contained certain words (including profanity), and did not contain hyperlinks or user mentions.

Text classification techniques are often used in combination with simple keyword and/or location filters to identify tweets related to a particular disaster. For example, the Emergency Situation Awareness tool (Robinson, Power, & Cameron, 2013a) classifies tweets containing the keywords "earthquake" or "#eqnz" to help identify tweets reporting a new earthquake event.

Clustering tweets into groups of similar tweets is another method of reducing the burden of reading individual tweets and to obtain a "sense" of the topics being discussed. By selecting a representative tweet or portion of text from each cluster for display, the user can quickly get an overview of the content of each tweet cluster.

2.2. Determining Location

During a disaster, the ability to attach precise locations to disaster-related tweets is vital but often difficult to do automatically. Methods of inferring the location of the tweet have been discussed in Chapter 1. An example of a tweet message containing location information is shown in Figure 6.7.[14]

Determining location is also an important task for earthquake detection (Robinson, Power, & Cameron, 2013b). If a sudden burst of tweets mentioning an earthquake originate from a relatively small geographic region, then it is a strong indicator that people are tweeting about feeling an earthquake. A large geographic spread of tweets mentioning an earthquake may be due to people reacting to news of an earthquake elsewhere in the world, or perhaps due to

---

[14] https://twitter.com/nixs579/status/296093672691363842/photo/1.

Nicole Tribe
@nixs579   ☼   ⚹ Follow

Water over road at end of nirimba street at
scrubby creek. pic.twitter.com/7DvHezZh

📍 from location

↰ Reply ⇄ Retweet ★ Favorite ••• More

2:13 PM - 29 Jan 2013   Flag media

Figure 6.7. Tweet with a location example.

people commenting on a television documentary on earthquakes. Figure 6.8 shows the difference in spread of tweets mentioning an earthquake as collected by the ESA system, which only collects tweets originating from Australia and New Zealand. Figure 6.8a corresponds to a small earthquake felt in Melbourne Australia, whereas Figure 6.8b shows the reaction to a large earthquake reported to have hit just off the Aceh Province in Indonesia.

2.3. *Trustworthy Tweets*

Trust is one of the biggest hurdles to overcome when it comes to using social media to monitor disasters. Historically, emergency management agencies have relied on verified information from official sources, with the only input from the public being via the emergency call centers, such as 000 in Australia

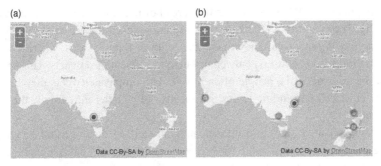

Figure 6.8. ESA heatmaps showing spread of earthquake tweets: (a) earthquake in Melbourne, Australia; (b) chat about an earthquake.

and 911 in the United States. While studies have found that the majority of disaster-related information posted by the public is truthful, there have been cases of false information being spread.

During a disaster, tweeters will often share third-party information related to the disaster, for example, a link to a weather forecast, news article, or image. Thomson et al. (2012) have examined source credibility of information shared via Twitter relating to the Fukushima disaster in Japan. Overall, they found that the profile anonymity of the tweeter influences their likelihood of sharing information from low-credibility sources. When they focused on Japanese language tweeters however, they found that while they were more anonymous (39.7 percent did not specify a profile location, compared to 24 percent for other languages), they referenced low-credibility sources less often than non-Japanese tweeters, which suggests that proximity to the disaster affects the likelihood of sharing low-credibility information.

High-credibility sources included traditional media, public institutions, enterprises, nongovernmental organizations (NGOs), nonprofit organizations (NPOs), freelance journalists, high-trust individuals, academics and professionals, and Fukushima locals. Low-credibility sources included unidentifiable individuals, nonlocals, conspiracy theorists, alternative media, and bots.

Mendoza, Poblete, and Castillo (2012) examined tweets related to the 2010 Chile earthquake disaster and found that propagation of tweets related to rumors versus reputable news differed. They used classification to determine whether a tweet affirms, denies, or questions the truth or rumor tweet. The authors found that 95.5 percent of tweets related to confirmed truths were classified as "affirm," with only 0.3 percent "denies." On the other hand, 50 percent of tweets related to false rumors were classified as "denies," with 13 percent as "questions."

Gupta et al. (2013) focused on the spread of fake images during Hurricane Sandy. They identified 10,350 tweets containing fake images, with 86 percent of these being retweets. They found that follower relationships, where Twitter users "follow" other users, only contributed 11 percent of retweets. This shows that in cases of crisis, people often retweet and propagate tweets they find in Twitter search or trending topics, irrespective of whether they follow the user or not.

Gupta et al. (2013) use classification models to distinguish fake photo tweets from real ones with 97 percent accuracy; their dataset included a high proportion of similar retweets; consequently, the accuracy is potentially inflated. Tweet-based features such as message text length, the presence of certain punctuation marks or emoticons (for example, an exclamation mark [!] or happy emoticon [:)]) were found to be effective, while user based-features such as number of friends or followers and the presence of a user's URL were not effective. They performed two-class classification using both Naive Bayes (Lewis, 1998) and Decision Tree (Lewis & Ringuette, 1994) classifiers.

Examples of misleading photos that circulated Twitter during Hurricane Sandy are shown in Figure 6.9. The first photo[15] in Figure 6.9a was of a 2011 thunderstorm during a tornado alert. Note the number of retweets and favorites for this tweet. The next photo[16] in Figure 6.9b was from the movie *The Day After Tomorrow*. The following example[17] in Figure 6.9c is a real photo, but it was not taken during the Sandy event. The final photo[18] in Figure 6.9d shows a shark swimming in a residential area that has been flooded. This image was Photoshopped.[19]

Myth busting was a key function carried out by the Queensland Police Service (QPS) social media team during the 2011 Queensland floods (Charlton, 2012). They were quickly able to quash rumors and misreporting before they became "fact" in the mainstream media, mainly through the #mythbuster hashtag. An example can be seen in Figure 6.10.[20] During these floods, rumors were being spread that the city's water supply was contaminated. This was not true, and the trusted authority of the QPS was able to reassure the community.

During Hurricane Sandy, the Federal Emergency Management Agency in the United States set up a rumor control site[21] to confirm or deny information that was circulating on social media. The rumor that the New York Stock Exchange

---

[15] https://twitter.com/jamster83/status/262869380117962752/photo/1.
[16] https://twitter.com/LaPointeDance/status/262977930022514688.
[17] https://twitter.com/OMGFacts/status/262955515401863168/photo/1.
[18] https://twitter.com/sista71/status/263034862338985986/photo/1.
[19] http://www.snopes.com/photos/natural/sandy.asp.
[20] https://twitter.com/QPSmedia/status/25382673950179329.
[21] http://www.fema.gov/hurricane-sandy-rumor-control

Figure 6.9. Examples of misleading Sandy photos.

trading floor was three feet underwater is a good example of how false information can spread via Twitter and in fact be reported as truth by mainstream media.
The original rumor tweet is shown in Figure 6.11.[22] The information in this tweet
was reported by both CNN and the Weather Channel before it was corrected by
CNBC just under an hour after the original tweet.[23]

The Boston bombing is another example of false information spreading via
Twitter, where the names of two people who were not connected to the case
were circulated as being prime suspects.[24] One of the names was allegedly

[22] https://twitter.com/ComfortablySmug/statuses/263083953152466947.
[23] http://www.washingtonpost.com/blogs/erik-wemple/post/hurricane-sandy-nyse-not
      -flooded/2012/10/30/37532512-223d-11e2-ac85-e669876c6a24_blog.html.
[24] http://www.theatlantic.com/technology/archive/2013/04/-bostonbombing-the-anatomy-of-a
      -misinformation-disaster/275155/.

Figure 6.10. A #mythbuster tweet by QPS during flooding event.

Figure 6.11. An example rumor tweet during Hurricane Sandy.

heard on a police scanner, and the other was of a missing Brown University student whom someone thought they recognized in photos of the event. Within 7 minutes of the first tweet to claim that the Boston Police Department (BDP) had identified the two suspects, the media started circulating the information. This information spread like wildfire, with it being tweeted and retweeted thousands of times before being corrected by NBC a few hours later.

2.4. *Event Detection*

Twitter can be used to identify when a disaster event has occurred. People in the affected area become human sensors who report events of interest. The problem remains how to reliably detect the high-value information from the deluge that surrounds it. In general, the most useful tweets come from the facts published by a small number of individuals located in close proximity to the location of the disaster. These tweets are rare and difficult to find.

A number of different techniques have been applied to this task of finding the needle in the haystack of tweets. This information can then be used as an early alert system that can be propagated through the use of retweets to amplify the message and by the construction of community-established hashtags.

In New Zealand, for example, the hashtag #eqnz became commonly referenced by New Zealanders in earthquake-related tweets. This occurred after a brief "hashtag war," with examples of the competing hashtags being #earthquake, #quakenz, #nzquake, and #christchurch. The "winner," #eqnz, was probably due to it being short, descriptive, easy to remember, and quick to type. The use of such commonly adopted hashtags make it relatively easy to identify tweets of interest using standard tweet search tools already available.

However, when the Twitter community does not adopt a hashtag that succinctly identifies a particular disaster, other tools are required. These are mostly based on machine learning techniques, natural language processing tools, and bursts of activity identified in the tweet stream.

Studies of tweets sent during crises and natural disasters have found that people send useful timely information about real-world events (Mendoza, Poblete, & Castillo, 2010). Natural Language Processing (NLP) classifiers have been used to extract situation awareness information, as reported by Verma et al. (2011). They found a strong correlation between data collected in a region about a local event and evidence of situation awareness tweet content.

Several systems have been developed for the automatic detection of earthquakes via Twitter. The Twitter Earthquake Detector (TED) from Earle, Bowden, & Guy (2012) describe a detection system operating over a filtered tweet stream. Their detector is adjustable, with a sensitivity measure based on a short-term-average, long-term-average algorithm with best results achieved using a "moderate" setting. They found that their detections were fast; about 75 percent occur within 2 minutes of the earthquake origin time, which is faster than seismograph detection in regions that are not well instrumented. They also found that the tweets provide a concise first impression from the people experiencing the earthquake.

Sakaki, Okazaki, and Matsuo (2010, 2013) have deployed an operational system in Japan that uses natural language processing techniques to classify tweets containing specific keywords, such as "earthquake" or "shaking." Positively classified tweets are then used to generate a probabilistic spatiotemporal model of the event, and particle filtering is used to estimate the earthquake location. Users of both systems are notified of a potential earthquake via email.

The ESA system described in Section 1.5 has been configured to identify earthquakes and fires. Earthquake detection was initially based on filtering earthquake-related keywords from the alerts generated by the system, combined with heuristics determined through analysis. An example of earthquake-related alerts can be seen in Figure 6.3.

In summary, when the tweets are identified as being close geographically and the retweet percentage is low, an email notification is generated. Once detected, an email notification containing the earthquake evidence from the tweet is sent to the Joint Australian Tsunami Warning Centre (JATWC) (Robinson, Power, & Cameron, 2013b).

This system was subsequently improved by introducing a classifier specifically trained to identify evidence of firsthand "felt" reports based on earthquake-related tweets. During its initial five months of operation, the system generated forty-nine notifications, of which twenty-nine related to real earthquake events. The average time delay between the earthquake origin time and when ESA sent a notification email was 3:03 (3 minutes and 3 seconds). This provides JATWC an additional means of early warning to alert it of the potential of an earthquake to augment its existing system based on seismic stations (Robinson, Power, & Cameron, 2013a).

The ESA system was also configured to identify fires reported on Twitter in Australia and New Zealand. Fire-related "alert words" identified by ESA were further processed by a classifier to determine whether they correspond to an actual fire event. This task was considerably more difficult than the earthquake detector due to the inherent ambiguity of fire-related alert words. The use of a classifier significantly increased the accuracy of the fire detector, from 48 percent to 78 percent; however, the recall score reduced from 1.0 to 0.8.

2.5. Seeking Help

Social media is growing in acceptance, as indicated by the 2012 American Red Cross survey,[25] which reports that 75 percent of the general public felt that national agencies should be monitoring social media, and 70 percent believe that local agencies should be monitoring social media. They also found that 36 percent of the general public expected help to arrive in less than one hour if they posted a request for help on social media. A further 40 percent expected help to arrive in one to three hours.

While many emergency agencies have become comfortable with distributing information via social media, evidence of agencies responding to calls for help via social media is far less common. An example where this has occurred was during Hurricane Sandy,[26] where a single staff member at the New York

---

[25] http://www.redcross.org/news/press-release/More-Americans-Using-Mobile-Apps-in-Emergencies.

[26] http://edition.cnn.com/2012/11/01/tech/social-media/twitter-fdny/.

Figure 6.12. A request for help via Twitter.

City Fire Department responded to hundreds of tweets requesting help, most of them in the first two hours after Sandy made landfall. The staff member commented:

> People were so scared they were reaching out to anyone they thought might listen. It really struck a chord with me. I tried to help them as best as I could. A lot of people couldn't get through to a 911 dispatcher. So I took their information and called our dispatchers myself to make sure they sent an emergency crew.

Figure 6.12[27] shows an Australian example where help was requested via Twitter. The response to this tweet demonstrates how agencies are reluctant to act on information not received via the usual channels. It should be noted that the tweeter in this instance is a journalist, and it is unclear as to how he was in contact with the family of the boy who needed help. The Baffle Creek township was completely isolated by floodwaters and cut off from telecommunications during the flooding event,[28] so it is unlikely the family could have made the call themselves.

2.6. *Community Engagement*

Immediately after an emergency or disaster event has occurred, Twitter has been used to seek assistance for those in need, as noted previously. People in

[27] https://twitter.com/DamonAM/status/296036323612057602.
[28] http://www.gladstoneobserver.com.au/news/operation-baffle-creek-accessing-inaccessible/1739006/.

the affected area also seek information about the event and the damage it has caused and to check on the well-being of people in the area. It is also used by others in the community not in the impacted area, but who are nevertheless interested to find out further information. In general, Twitter is used to send out requests for help, spread rumors and news by retweets, and seek further information about the evolving situation.

The use of Twitter in this way is a means of sharing in the experience with others who are similarly concerned and as a way of seeking support from others as a form of self-help or as a pseudocounseling service to share feelings and seek comfort and support, referred to as psychological first aid.

In Japan, Twitter have introduced a Lifeline service[29] that helps users find critical information during a crisis. Users can use their postal code to find and follow local accounts that are important during an emergency, such as those managed by government agencies, the media, and utility companies.

Twitter has also introduced a Twitter Alert service,[30] where users can sign up to receive an account's Twitter Alerts, which are delivered via Short Message Service (SMS) or Twitter mobile apps. Accounts that can publish Twitter Alerts include those managed by local, national, and international institutions that provide critical information to the general public. These include law enforcement and public safety agencies; emergency management agencies; city and municipal governments; country and regional agencies; and select state, federal, and national agencies and NGOs.

In Australia, the Queensland Police Service (QPS) has been an early adopter of social media for public engagement and emergency disaster responsiveness. Charlton (2012) describes how the QPS successfully made use of social media during several natural disasters in 2011. The department used a combination of social media channels: Facebook, Twitter, and YouTube, with most of their posts being sent to both Facebook and Twitter, with hashtags added to the tweets. Key points of media conferences were tweeted live, and myth busting of misinformation and rumors was another important service they provided.

The QPS media team were prepared for uptake of social media because the team had just undergone a seven-month trial, which meant that their staff were familiar with the tools and were able to cope when the first disaster was declared and their Twitter followers and Facebook "likes" skyrocketed. After the 2011 Toowoomba flash flood, their "likes" increased from seventeen thousand to one hundred thousand in twenty-four hours. Given that the majority of the information the QPS released was factual and in the interests of public safety, it was

---

[29] https://blog.twitter.com/2012/a-new-lifeline-in-japan.
[30] https://blog.twitter.com/2013/twitter-alerts-critical-information-when-you-need-it-most.

released immediately, without having to go through a time-consuming formal clearance process. The media team was trusted to use its judgment. Within days of the first disaster, not only were mainstream media relying on the QPS social media accounts as a key source of information, they were actively referring the public to the QPS social media channels. QPS tweets appeared in national TV networks news tickers and were read out by radio station announcers within moments of the media team publishing them. The social media team provided 24/7 moderation of the QPS social media accounts, responding to inquiries from the public where possible.

Social media also played a significant role during the Hurricane Sandy event. Chatfield, Scholl, and Brajawidagda (2014) examined how the government engaged with citizens through social media channels during and after the event. They analyzed 132,922 #sandy tweets from a nineteen-day period and noted that government agencies, mass media, and weather information providers were the top #sandy tweeters. The authors carried out a social network analysis of particular tweets issued by the government agencies responsible for disaster response management and found that citizen co-production and message amplification via retweeting greatly extended their ability to provide critical and essential public information services in a timely fashion. One tweet in particular issued by the New York City Fire Department (FDNY) about the opening of shelters spread quickly during the two hours immediately after the initial tweet, reaching significantly more Twitter users than FDNY's direct followers.

It was also noted that when the emergency services (911) and nonurgent municipal services (311) call systems became overwhelmed, Twitter became the only multidirectional interactive communications channel available. Agencies were able to collect critical information in real time directly from communities, businesses, and individuals that would otherwise not have been available. As discussed in Section 2.5, the FDNY even went to the extent of dispatching help requested via Twitter[26], which received much praise from citizens on Twitter. In contrast, the general public expressed frustration at the increased average wait times for the city government's traditional 911 and 311 two-way communication channels.

3. Discussion

Case studies have been reported (Stollberg & de Groeve, 2012; Beneito-Montagut et al., 2013) that demonstrate the importance of placing social media information in the correct context. Emergency managers operate under a command-and-control structure, and while drivers exist to embrace this new technology to improve situation awareness, there are still barriers to adoption based on organizational constraints. These barriers will be overcome with the increasing acceptance of social media, so long as the veracity of this information is suitably characterized.

Twitter has been used successfully to identify emergency events, obtain crowdsourced information as the event unfolds, provide up-to-date information to the affected community from authoritative agencies, and aid with resource planning. The survey of existing tools and technologies and the case studies described in this chapter demonstrate that Twitter is an effective source of public information for situational awareness for emergency managers and crisis coordinators and is also a useful means of engaging with the community during disaster response and recovery activities.

The opportunities of using Twitter for disaster monitoring and response are noted in the following section, and Section 3.2 discusses the limitations that remain. This is followed by a description of further work required to ensure the widespread adoption of the effective use of Twitter for disaster response.

3.1. *Future Opportunities*

The future role of social media for emergency service agencies requires careful consideration in order to manage this new communication channel effectively. There is a general expectation in the community that emergency services will actively engage on a range of social media platforms. The increased use by the public to report incidents on Twitter and to seek specific information from authoritative sources is an extra task expected of these agencies. This will require new infrastructure and resourcing in addition to that traditionally provided.

The public expect to be provided with warnings, advice, and up-to-date information in times of emergency. This information needs to be provided through traditional media channels and social media platforms, which places an expectation on the emergency services organizations to deliver near–real-time updates on the evolving situation for all emergency types, such as bushfires, severe storms, floods, and so on.

Social media must remain one of several channels through which to reach and communicate with people. Social media needs to work effectively alongside traditional methods of communication, such as television, radio, and telephone.

These operational changes need to be supported by new policies that recognize and accommodate the role of social media for emergency management purposes. These policies will guide staff and volunteers about their responsibilities when using social media for operational purposes.

As with all forms of communication from emergency service organizations about emergency events, the use of Twitter needs to maintain trust with the community. This is done by providing accurate information in a timely manner using transparent processes on information platforms that are accessible to a wide cross section of the community and that maintain consistency of the information provided.

This should not be considered a new burden, but an opportunity. Social media can offer increased efficiency with its ability to reach more people with fewer resources. One solution to achieve such efficiencies is through the use of a single message disseminated via various information channels through a single information management mechanism.

Social media needs to be considered in all elements of the disaster management lifecycle, from prevention (informing the community about ongoing mitigation tasks such as hazard reduction burns), preparedness (providing up-to-date information about imminent emergency events), response (public information being used by response agencies), and recovery (providing advice and support where needed). These benefits allow everyone involved in emergencies, from the response agencies to the affected community, to be more resilient in the face of emergency situations and better equipped to handle events when they occur and to recover faster.

There is evidence that people who consider themselves part of a community are better able to manage disaster events and work effectively together and recover faster. Digital communities are just as relevant in this respect as physical communities.

The aim for disaster monitoring is to utilize tools and technologies that provide near–real-time monitoring of Twitter to improve the situational awareness of emergency events for emergency managers and crisis coordinators.

3.2. *Limitations*

There are a number of issues still to be resolved, as outlined in this chapter. These issues are mostly concerned about how to manage sensibly the large volume of information to identify high-value tweets, how to summarize and visualize relevant information when found, and how to ensure reliability of the tweet content. These are ongoing issues and there are tools available that go some way to addressing this, as noted in this chapter.

Regardless of the best efforts of preparation and planning, disasters always involve situations not previously considered. The use of social media needs to be utilized in an effective way to ameliorate the situation, not exacerbate it. This will require strong commitment from the emergency services agencies to dedicate resources to monitor social media; provide regular, informative, targeted content to those seeking it; respond to direct inquiries and calls for help; and to validate and verify the information rapidly as it becomes available.

As the use of social media becomes more widespread, it will require social media staff to be employed within organizations. Currently, these functions are being performed by dedicated staff who have an interest and good understanding of social media, but this cannot be relied upon. Issues regarding staffing and the corresponding financial implications will need to be addressed. There is also the potential for the development of new technology, either embracing or extending existing platforms or adopting the next big "thing" in this rapidly changing landscape of applications and tools.

The use of Twitter is not a separate tool but one that needs to be integrated into existing work practices. For example, how should agencies respond to a call for help published on Twitter? This has occurred in isolated instances; refer to the example during Hurricane Sandy described in Section 2.5. However, the response from the Queensland State Emergency Service (SES) to the request for help shown in Figure 6.12 directed the service to use the traditional channel. In times of crisis, these normal communications channels can be stressed, resulting in calls not being answered. The work practices of these agencies are yet to embrace new methods of supporting the public in this way.

A number of other limitations for using Twitter for disaster monitoring remain. Some are specific to this domain, for example, the use of consistent terminology to describe different emergency events in way that is clear to the community. Others are significant for all Twitter users, such as developing reliable methods to identify genuine content reported on Twitter from false alarms and malicious reporting.

The use of Twitter targets specific people in the community. The devices required to use social media, typically smart phones, tablets, and computers, are not generally available to disadvantaged groups, some members of minority or multicultural groups, the elderly, and those who live in areas of poor connectivity. These sections of the community will not be part of the Twitter conversation, so traditional methods of communication need to be maintained.

Privacy and confidentiality aspects of Twitter need to be considered. Twitter content is under the control of the user who produces it, and yet users are sometimes surprised when people other than their friends and followers respond to their tweets. These issues need to be carefully considered and guidelines put in place to provide guidance to official users of authoritative Twitter accounts.

As social media becomes more entwined in our daily lives, our dependence on this communication channel may in itself become a hindrance during times of disasters. The tools used to connect to our digital communities rely on infrastructure, power supply, and the Internet, which will certainly be affected in times of crises.

3.3. *Future Work*

What other gaps will real-time social media fill as we work toward safer, sustainable communities? The case studies presented in this chapter will help professional emergency managers and crisis coordinators understand the state of the art in tools, techniques, issues, and challenges in engaging with communities using near–real-time social media throughout the PPRR spectrum of activities.

Approaches to filter, analyze, condense, and summarize tweets address the challenges of identifying valuable information and reducing the potential information overload: there are too many tweets to read them all.

Techniques for extracting location cues from tweet content add confidence in reported locations of events and incidents. These tools and techniques have variable success and will need improvement.

Understanding the trustworthiness of a tweet remains a challenge. Content classification approaches have been shown to be successful. But as research has shown, users are likely to have come across questionable tweets by using native search services. Perhaps user-driven veracity voting will help the Twitter community provide feedback on questionable content.

Approaches to event detection have been applied in locations of small-area scale through to nationwide scale. The challenges for event detection are to develop real-time algorithms capable of operating simultaneously in multiple dimensions of space, time, and content and from small-area scale through global-scale.

During the impact phase of a disaster, help-seeking requests and infrastructure status are seen as high-value information for emergency management teams. Classifiers to identify help-seeking requests and infrastructure status face a trade-off in terms of development time/complexity versus the utility of directly searching for information.

Twitter is used for emergency and disaster monitoring. There is evidence that emergency and disaster management agencies are adapting their work functions and team structures to exploit social media channels (Teague, McLeod, & Pascoe, 2010; AFAC, 2013).

There are many potential threads for future work. In the context of professional emergency management and crisis coordination teams, the near-term focus likely remains on (a) understanding what other types of social media information are valuable to their awareness of a situation; (b) developing fit-for-purpose tools to filter, analyze, condense, and summarize social media content; (c) further developing tools to fuse, compare, and contrast information from social media content feeds and other authoritative content feeds; (d) making fit-for-purpose tools that enable community engagement while supporting incident management team requirements to log community engagements in support of post-incident analysis; and (e) developing the next generation of tools that are tuned to information and situation awareness needs at scales from an individual watch officer to an incident management team to a nationwide federated emergency and disaster management enterprise.

References

Abel, Fabian, Hauff, Claudia, Houben, Geert-Jan, Stronkman, Richard, and Tao, Ke. (2012). Twitcident: fighting fire with information from social web streams. In *WWW (Companion Volume)*, ed. Alain Mille, Fabien L. Gandon, Jacques Misselis, Michael Rabinovich, and Steffen Staab (pp. 305–8). ACM.

AFAC. (2013). *The Australiasian Inter-Service Incident Management System*, 4th ed. Australiasian Fire and Emergency Service Authorities Council.

Anderson, Martin. (2012). Integrating social media into traditional management command and control structures: the square peg into the round hole. In *Australian and New Zealand Disaster and Emergency Management Conference*, ed. Peter Sugg (pp. 18–34). AST Management Pty Ltd.

Beneito-Montagut, Roser, Anson, Susan, Shaw, Duncan, and Brewster, Christopher. (2013). Resilience: two case studies on governmental social media use for emergency communication. In *Proceedings of the Information Systems for Crisis Response and Management Conference (ISCRAM 2013 12–15 May, 2013)* (pp. 828–33). ISCRAM.

Cameron, Mark A., Power, Robert, Robinson, Bella, and Yin, Jie. (2012). Emergency situation awareness from Twitter for crisis management. In *Proceedings of the 21st International Conference Companion on World Wide Web. WWW '12 Companion* (pp. 695–8). ACM.

Charlton, Kym. (2012). *Disaster Management and Social Media – A Case Study*. Tech. rept. Media and Public Affairs Branch, Queensland Police Service. Accessed April 26, 2013.

Chatfield, Akemi Takeoka, Scholl, Hans Jochen, and Brajawidagda, Uuf. (2014). #Sandy tweets: citizens' co-production of time-critical information during an unfolding catastrophe. In *2014 47th Hawaii International Conference on System Sciences*, 1947–57.

Chowdhury, Soudip Roy, Imran, Muhammad, Asghar, Muhammad Rizwan, Amer-Yahia, Sihem, and Castillo, Carlos. (2013). Tweet4act: using incident-specific profiles for classifying crisis-related messages. In *The 10th International Conference on Information Systems for Crisis Response and Management (ISCRAM)* (pp. 834–9) ISCRAM.

Earle, Paul S., Bowden, Daniel C., and Guy, Michelle. (2012). Twitter earthquake detection: earthquake monitoring in a social world. *Annals of GeoPhysics*, 54(6), 708–15.

Endsley, Mica R. (1995). Toward a theory of situation awareness in dynamic systems: situation awareness. *Human Factors*, 37(1), 32–64.

Guha-Sapir, Debby, Vos, Femke, and Below, Regina, with Ponserre, Sylvain. (2011). *Annual Disaster Statistical Review 2010: The Numbers and Trends*. Centre for Research on the Epidemiology of Disasters. http://www.cred.be/sites/default/files/ADSR_2010.pdf.

Gupta, Aditi, Lamba, Hemank, Kumaraguru, Ponnurangam, and Joshi, Anupam. (2013). Faking Sandy: characterizing and identifying fake images on Twitter during Hurricane Sandy. In *Proceedings of the 22nd International Conference on World Wide Web Companion. WWW '13 Companion* (pp. 729–36). International World Wide Web Conferences Steering Committee.

Hawkins, Charlie, Prakash, Mahesh, Sullivan, Andrew, Box, Paul, Cameron, Mark, Power, Robert, Gould, Jim, Dunstall, Simon, and Dormer, Alan. (2012). *All Hazards: Digital Technology & Services for Disaster Management*. Tech. rept. CSIRO, ePublush # EP128826.

Heinzelman, Jessica, and Waters, Carol. (2010). *Crowdsourcing Crisis Information in Disaster-Affected Haiti*. Tech. rept. United States Institute of Peace.

Imran, Muhammad, Castillo, Carlos, Lucas, Ji, Meier, Patrick, and Rogstadius, Jakob. (2014). Coordinating human and machine intelligence to classify microblog communications in crises. In *The 11th International Conference on Information Systems for Crisis Response and Management (ISCRAM)* (pp. 712–21). ISCRAM.

Imran, Muhammad, Elbassuoni, Shady Mamoon, Castillo, Carlos, Diaz, Fernando, and Meier, Patrick. (2013). Extracting information nuggets from disaster-related messages in social media. In *The 10th International Conference on Information Systems for Crisis Response and Management (ISCRAM)* (pp. 791–800). ISCRAM.

Joachims, Thorsten. (1998). Text categorization with support vector machines: learning with many relevant features. In *Proceedings of the 10th European Conference on Machine Learning. ECML '98* (pp. 137–42). Springer-Verlag.

Lewis, David D. (1998). Naive (Bayes) at forty: the independence assumption in information retrieval. In *Machine Learning: ECML-98* (pp. 4–15). Springer.

Lewis, David D., and Ringuette, Marc. (1994). A comparison of two learning algorithms for text categorization. In *Third Annual Symposium on Document Analysis and Information Retrieval*, vol. 33 (pp. 81–93). Information Science Research Institute, University of Nevada.

Lindsay, Bruce R. (2011). *Social Media and Disasters: Current Uses, Future Options, and Policy Considerations*. Tech. rept. Analyst in American National Government. http://www.fas.org/sgp/crs/homesec/R41987.pdf (Accessed March 12, 2013).

Mendoza, Marcelo, Poblete, Barbara, and Castillo, Carlos. (2010). Twitter under crisis: can we trust what we RT? In *Proceedings of the First Workshop on Social Media Analytics. SOMA '10* (pp. 71–9). ACM.

Nigam, Kamal, Lafferty, John, and McCallum, Andrew. (1999). Using maximum entropy for text classification. In *IJCAI-99 Workshop on Machine Learning for Information Filtering*, vol. 1 (pp. 61–7). IJCAI.

Robinson, Bella, Power, Robert, and Cameron, Mark. (2013a). An evidence based earthquake detector using Twitter. In *Proceedings of the Workshop on Language*

Processing and Crisis Information 2013 (pp. 1–9). Asian Federation of Natural Language Processing.

Robinson, Bella, Power, Robert, and Cameron, Mark. (2013b). A sensitive Twitter earthquake detector. In *Proceedings of the 22nd international conference on World Wide Web Companion. WWW '13 Companion* (pp. 999–1002). International World Wide Web Conferences Steering Committee.

Rogstadius, Jakob, Vukovic, Maja, Teixeira, Claudio A., Kostakos, Vassilis, Karapanos, Evangelos, and Laredo, Jim A. (2013). CrisisTracker: crowdsourced social media curation for disaster awareness. *IBM Journal of Research and Development*, 57(5), 4:1–4:13.

Sakaki, Takeshi, Okazaki, Makoto, and Matsuo, Yutaka. (2010). Earthquake shakes Twitter users: real-time event detection by social sensors. In *Proceedings of the 19th International Conference on World Wide Web. WWW '10* (pp. 851–60). ACM.

Sakaki, Takeshi, Okazaki, Makoto, and Matsuo, Yutaka. (2013). Tweet analysis for real-time event detection and earthquake reporting system development. *IEEE Transactions on Knowledge and Data Engineering*, 25(4), 919–31.

Schulz, Axel, and Ristoski, Petar. (2013). The car that hit the burning house: understanding small scale incident related information in microblogs. In *Seventh International AAAI Conference on Weblogs and Social Media* (pp. 11–14). AAAI.

Schulz, Axel, Ristoski, Petar, and Paulheim, Heiko. (2013). I see a car crash: real-time detection of small scale incidents in microblogs. In *The Semantic Web: ESWC 2013 Satellite Events*. Lecture Notes in Computer Science, no. 7955, ed. Philipp Cimiano, Miriam Fernàndez, Vanessa Lopez, Stefan Schlobach, and Johanna Völker (pp. 22–33). Springer Berlin Heidelberg.

Stephenson, Catherine, Handmer, John, and Haywood, Aimee. (2012). *Estimating the net cost of the 2009 Black Saturday Fires to the affected regions*. Tech. rept. RMIT, Bushfire CRC, Victorian DSE.

Stollberg, Beate, and de Groeve, Tom. (2012). The use of social media within the global disaster alert and coordination system (GDACS). In *Proceedings of the 21st International Conference Companion on World Wide Web. WWW '12 Companion* (pp. 703–6). ACM.

Teague, Bernard, McLeod, Ronald, and Pascoe, Susan. (2010). *2009 Victorian Bushfires Royal Commission: Final Report*. Parliament of Victoria.

Thomson, Robert, Ito, Naoya, Suda, Hinako, Lin, Fangyu, Liu, Yafei, Hayasaka, Ryo, Isochi, Ryuzo, and Wang, Zian. (2012). Trusting tweets: the Fukushima disaster and information source credibility on Twitter. In *The 9th International Conference on Information Systems for Crisis Response and Management (ISCRAM)*. http://www.iscramlive.org/ISCRAM2012/proceedings/112.pdf.

Verma, Sudha, Vieweg, Sarah, Corvey, William, Palen, Leysia, Martin, James H., Palmer, Martha, Schram, Aaron, and Anderson, Kenneth Mark. (2011). Natural language processing to the rescue? Extracting "situational awareness" tweets during mass emergency. In *ICWSM*, ed. Lada A. Adamic, Ricardo A. Baeza-Yates, and Scott Counts (pp. 385–92). AAAI.

Index